1988 TRANSCRIPTS

Beer and Brewing
VOLUME 8

NATIONAL CONFERENCE
ON QUALITY BEER AND BREWING

Talks By

Charlie Papazian

Michael Jackson

Daniel Carey

Dr. George Fix

Jean Guinard/
Ian Robertson

David Miller

Randy Mosher

Prince Luitpold
von Bayern

Leon Havill

Henrik Bachofen
von Echt

Hans Bilger

Charlie Papazian/
Greg Noonan

Edited by Virginia Thomas
Brewers Publications

Beer and Brewing, Vol. 8
Edited by Virginia Thomas
Copyright 1988 by Association of Brewers

ISBN 0-937381-11-X
Printed in the United States of America

Published by Brewers Publications
a division of the Association of Brewers
P.O. Box 287, Boulder, Colorado 80306 USA
Tel. (303) 447-0816

Direct all inquiries/orders to the above address.

Cover design by David Bjorkman

Interior Photos by David Bjorkman, National News Service

Contents

Acknowledgments

Special thanks to the following companies who assisted financially in the production of this book:

Adolph Coors Company,
Golden, Colorado

Anchor Brewing Company,
San Francisco, California

Anheuser-Busch, Inc.,
St. Louis, Missouri

Boston Beer Company,
Jamaica Plain, Massachusetts

John I. Haas, Inc.,
Yakima, Washington

Krones, Inc.,
Franklin, Wisconsin

Miller Brewing Company,
Milwaukee, Wisconsin

Foreword

The twelve chapters included in this book were presented originally as talks at the Conference on Quality Beer and Brewing in Denver, Colorado, in June 1988. As in past years, transforming these presentations into this volume on brewing has been one of the most satisfying projects we have done here at Brewers Publications.

As the editor of this book, I particularly enjoy working with the material unique to each speaker. I try to preserve the flavor, the enthusiasm, and the character of each individual, while changing the spoken word into the written word (an almost completely different form of the English language). Of course, accuracy is paramount, and in almost every case, the authors have read their talks after transcription and made changes and additions.

This volume of Beer and Brewing is especially interesting because of the diverse range of topics it covers. To me, it is a perfect match to the unique combination of technical and aesthetic interests that converge in beer brewers and lovers. The information on hop oils that is presented here by Dr. George Fix represents the cutting edge of research to help brewers. The opinions of the forward-thinking Prince Luitpold are uniquely poised between brewing history (his ancestor Wilhelm IV made the Reinheitsgebot Purity Law) and the trends of the future (brewpubs in the Eastern Bloc). Michael Jackson's campaign for cooking with beer and selecting beers to accompany and complement various foods is a service to beer-lovers everywhere. Dan  Carey's formulation of a Maibock and Randy Mosher's development of brewers' worksheets fit perfectly into the brewer's kitchen. And Leon Havill's humorous look at the history of mead is as welcome as a glass of clear, still mead.

I want to thank David Bjorkman, National News Service photographer, for his outstanding photos in this book. They provide an intimate glimpse of the Conference and its speakers.

I also thank Lois Canaday for her help in keeping me on the straight and narrow in avoiding typographical and semantic errors.

Last, I thank the authors for caring enough about the readers of this book to review and correct the written copy that appears here.

Virginia Thomas
Boulder, Colorado

1.
Ten Years of Homebrewing

Charlie Papazian
American Homebrewers Association

About ten years ago in Boulder, Colorado, I started teaching classes on homebrewing. First I gave my students a beer to drink. Then, I taught them to make beer. I told them that beer is made from from water, malted barley, yeast, and hops. Mix those all together, let them ferment for a few weeks, and you have beer. Then I gave them another beer. Today I would like to talk about the American Homebrewers Association and my involvement with beer-making.

My first experience with homebrewing was in 1970 when I was going to school at the University of Virginia and someone invited me to try some homebrew. It tasted pretty good—better than I thought it would taste—so I asked for the recipe. It read :

For Five Gallons
One can of Pabst Blue Ribbon Malt

One and a half pounds of sugar, white or black
One cake of yeast
Ferment until the bubbling stops, from seven days to five weeks.

In those days before I found out about corn sugar and brewer's yeast, most of my beer went down the drain. But when I got the hang of brewing, my college roommates and I had lots of parties with all the homebrew we made. After I graduated from school, I moved to Colorado and founded what was called the Log Boom Brewery. I began teaching classes on homebrewing through the Community Free School, where I taught for ten years. Once, I got a grant from the school for thirty dollars for experimentation and that launched my first log book. Until that point I had kept a few notes, but when I got the grant, I had to account for the money and the results of the experiment. My first project was the Triple Beam, in which I used oats, rice, and corn, and weighed things on a Triple Beam balance.

I made great beers in those days. One of them was an experiment made from a recipe I found in Mother Earth News. The recipe was for "Rootbeer" and I made it into "MackJack Rootbeer," an infamous brew. I couldn't figure out from the recipe why, if I put sugar, water, and rootbeer flavoring into the bottle with the yeast, the bottle wouldn't explode. I bottled the rootbeer in Champagne bottles and then lined some storage boxes with plastic and put them under the cupboard in case anything happened. Inevitably, the pressure grew in the bottles and they started exploding. One of them sheared off at the bottom, rocketed out of the box, and dented the underside of the cabinet where I had put them. After a few weeks, I opened a bottle and the uncorking managed to drench all four walls, the ceiling and the floor.

After that when I wanted a rootbeer, I would don my rainsuit, glasses, and leather gloves, announce that I was going to open a bottle of rootbeer and gingerly approach the case of bottles. By then, the legend had spread and everyone was prepared. One evening in October when the moon was full and twenty-five people had gathered at our place for a party, I put on my leather cap and goggles, looking for all the world like a World War I flying ace. I climbed onto the table, opened the bottle, and shimmering globs of rootbeer fluoresced in the moonlight then disastrously descended upon the onlookers as the entire contents of the bottle emptied in half a second. I remember the sound of the oohs and aahs. It was like the Fourth of July during the fireworks until the globs of rootbeer descended upon them. There were screams of horror as they fled.

I have learned quite a bit since then. My introduction to homebrew literature was through a young, debonnaire guy named Fred Eckhardt. His book, and another book by a young guy named Byron Burch, comprised

Charlie Papazian's experimental Brewery.

virtually all the homebrew literature in those days. I also sought out the British books: *Big Book of Brewing, Advanced Homebrewing,* and *Homebrew Beer Styles.* Those five books were my foundation for brewing.

In 1976, I published my first book, *Joy of Brewing.* It was a compilation of recipes and things I had learned from teaching homebrewing classes. I taught about one hundred people a year how to brew beer, which over a ten-year period amounted to about a thousand people. There was a certain spirit that developed in the classes over the years. All of them ended with a feast where we drank the homebrew we had made in class. Our parties were pretty special. In fact, some people purposely flunked the course. Finally, after a number of years, Beer and Steer developed from these parties. Charlie Matzen, a fellow who had taken my class, and I decided to roast a pig and have a homebrew party. In 1973, we invited our friends and fellow homebrewers to a festival in the mountains. That set the precedent. After that, we usually held Beer and Steer in the mountains where we had to run an electrical extension cord a quarter of a mile and truck the beer in a week ahead of time to let it settle. It was a mini-Woodstock. We made a hot tub for fifty people with bales of straw set in a circle and covered with plastic. One year we the mistake of building the hot tub out of hay, instead of straw, and the cows came in and ate it.

Around that time, I started the American Homebrew Association. I was a teacher in a private school then and had the summers off. I traveled during those months, always seeking good homebrew. One year, I hiked to the end of a logging road in a rainforest in British Columbia. At the end of the road was a cabin where a guy and his wife made homebrew after packing the malt fifteen miles. I stayed with them for several days, helping to collect rainwater for the beer.

On Bali in Indonesia I was walking down a path when I came across some people who offered me home-made palm toddy wine. On Fiji, I went to some small islands three hundred miles from the main group and stayed with a man and his ten kids for ten days. We began talking about homebrew, and he said, "You like home-brew? Tomorrow we'll have homebrew."

"Why can't we have it now?" I asked.

"Because we have to make it," he said.

We put boiled casava roots, sugar and water in a five-gallon crock with a full two cups of baker's yeast. The mixture bubbled and agitated, and we drank it the next day.

In 1977, I was introduced to Michael Jackson's *World Guide to Beer,* which provided me with inspiration and a seductive introduction to another way of thinking about beer. It was in that book that I learned about Rauch beer, cherry beer, and bock. In that year, Charlie Matzen and I traveled to Lake Powell in Utah over spring break, and I suggested putting out a homebrew newsletter. We spent a lot of time drinking beer and thinking about the idea. We decided that it was a good idea, but that if we were going to do it, we really would need to commit ourselves to it. We mulled it over for a year, and then in the spring break of 1978, we walked into the desert and asked, "What is the meaning of life?" A vision came to us that said, "Homebrew."

We started *zymurgy* and one of our first articles

was a reprint that had appeared in 1936. The odd coincidence was that the author of the article was the father of Kathy McClurg, a good friend of mine who is still managing editor with *zymurgy* after ten years. In that first issue, we also ran an article about Charlie Matzen's and my adventure in Hawaii and chronicled a five-gallon batch of beer that cost us one hundred dollars to brew.

In the second issue of *zymurgy*, Professor Surfeit made his debut. We also received a letter from Senator Alan Cranston of California congratulating us,
"Dear *zymurgy*,
Thank you for sending me a copy of *zymurgy*. I like it even if I can't pronounce it. Best of Luck."

In 1979, we sponsored our first National Homebrew Competition and held our first conference for budding homebrewers. Our first score sheet for the National Competition reflected the level of sophistication about homebrew at that time. Some of the remarks were:
Presentation: attractive, unattractive
Appearance: very clear, hazy
Bouquet: outrageous, wretched
Flavor: Too sour, sweet, oily, bitter, yeasty, skunky, rancid.
Body: full, limp
Yeast: not a trace, slime, sticks to tongue
After-taste: pleasant, mouth-wash is needed.
Not quite the sophistication we have these days.

In that year, homebrew clubs began springing up. The Maltose Falcons from California was the first club we heard from. Also, Aleford, the turkey, became our mascot and appeared in the third issue of *zymurgy* with a quote from a friend: "I wouldn't be here today if it weren't for the American Homebrewers." We chose the turkey as our official symbol because Ben Franklin wanted the turkey to become the American bird and we thought nothing was more American than a turkey.

We were still doing a lot of experimentation in those days. I taught school as a full-time job, put *zymurgy* together in my spare time, and traveled during my vacations. Charlie Matzen and I wrote an article about our research on taking homebrew with us on our trips. It appeared in the Summer *zymurgy* 1979 under the name, "Traveling with Homebrew."

"After years of exhausting research into the effects of homebrew on vacations, we assert that it is not only easy but practical to take homebrew along—even to remote areas.

"There are distinct advantages. Most of us need some time for our nervous systems to leave the working world worries behind. Homebrew is the fastest method we know of. Homebrew is also very effective in keeping your mind off those worries until the moment you must return. A delicious brew will make instant friends—a much better way to say hello than with a stick of gum.

"If you plan to backpack, remember that alcohol is lighter than water. It's an excellent mosquito repellent, or at least it helps you forget about them. Homebrew is also terrific for repelling/forgetting centipedes, scorpions, rattlesnakes, cockroaches, ants, wind, rain, snow and flat tires. In short homebrew makes the good parts of traveling better, and the lousy times tolerable.

"The type of beer (you need) depends on where you're going. Dark beer in the desert absorbs heat—light ales and lagers don't get hot as quickly. A variety is usually best so you can choose the right brew to accompany your mood or food."

This was the first mention of food/mood in *zymurgy*—a milestone

In 1980 *zymurgy* had its first article on microbrewers. In those days, only four existed: Cartwright Brewing in Portland, Debakker Brewing and New Albion Brewing in California, and Boulder Brewing in Boulder, Colorado. Over the years, the American Homebrewers Association has had tremendous support from large breweries such as the Adolph Coors Company, Anheuser-Busch, Millers, and Strohs. One day when we were still putting the magazine together in an office on my backporch, I decided to call Fritz Maytag, whom I had heard of but had never met. He came on the phone and we talked about microbrewing. He was incredibly helpful about how homebrewers could benefit the emerging microbrewing industry.

I also received a call from Matthew Reich, who later started New Amsterdam Brewing. He said, "I'm a homebrewer, and I want to start a brewery." And seven years later, he did.

We began doing interviews with interesting people and published an article about a homebrewer in Maine. We called it "Getting Useless in Eustis." It gives an idea of what homebrewing was like during Prohibition. We have tried to play down that part of our history, but clearly we should never forget our roots and the early years in which our forefathers struggled.

In later years we began having articles by Dr.

The Maltose Falcons in California was one of the first homebrew clubs to contact the American Homebrewers Association. Several Falcons attended the Tenth Anniversary wearing their Colors.

Michael Lewis and Al Andrews. In 1981, we held our first real homebrewers' conference in Chautauqua Park, in Boulder, Colorado. It was a small gathering of forty people including Pat Baker, Fred Eckhardt, and Michael Jackson. Two or three microbrewers also attended. It was at that conference that Michael Jackson came up with his famous quote, "We all lead a substantially diminished life when the beers we drink aren't as distinctive as Velveeta cheese on Wonder Bread."

It was at that conference that Hughes Rudd of ABC News and his staff prepared a news video on homebrewers. The script went something like this:

"We didn't have to go to Boulder, Colorado, just to see people drink beer, but we did go there to see them drink something that we thought went out with Prohibition— homebrewed beer. Homebrew, children, was quite popular during those years when alcoholic beverages were illegal in this country. But beer became legal in the early Thirties, so why were people still making it at home? These are homebrew fanatics, that's why.

"'Beer is malt, hops, water and love. And the love is the part that is being forgotten now,' said one avid brewer.

"There's even an American Homebrewers Association with about twelve hundred members, and they estimate that there are one million people in the country who make their own beer. During the two-hour cooking process, it may look like sewage, but after six weeks of fermentation, the homebrewers think it's nectar. One brewer named Whitey says it doesn't even explode in the basement any more like real Prohibition homebrew did, usually while the preacher was paying a call. Whitey also makes wine, and he says that will explode.

"'I was sleeping right above it. It was under the bed. I thought it was the end of the world,' he said.

"The annual convention is held in conjunction with a tasting contest to pick the best homebrews in the country whether they are Pilseners, lagers, ales, or whatever the brewmaker's fertile mind can ferment into being. The judging is tough.

"'This is weird. It's like Ralph Nader's safety beer,' said a brewer.

"In two days of filming, we didn't hear a single burp, not even at the banquet. They did get a little out of hand that night, however. One fellow turned up on the platform wearing an Arab headdress, although Arabs aren't known as beer-lovers, and then he drank beer out of a miniature bathtub.

"The Grand prize winner wasn't present, so someone dressed up as a chicken accepted the trophy. The official emblem of the association is a turkey because the members think there is nothing more American than a turkey, but they couldn't find a turkey suit, so they threw in the chicken. Details like that don't bother homebrew lovers. They go for the basic things in life.

"'Relax, don't worry, have a homebrew,' said Charlie Papazian, founder of the organization. 'That's what it takes to be a winner. And I know that for a fact.'"

In 1981, I traveled to England where I really learned a lot about brewing. I discovered Pale Ale, the Great British Beer Festival, real ale, and brewpubs. I visited Munton and Fison, Edme, Paines, Geordie, and Itona where I learned the malt-making process. When I returned, I had a much better understanding about how beer and malt extract are made. A significant thing I learned was that beer could be made, brewed, and drank within ten days. Until I traveled in England, I thought homebrew had to age for two or three months. In the Guinness Brewery, I was really surprised to discover that the beer I was drinking in the pub was only ten days old from when it was brewed. My articles appeared in *zymurgy*, and I believe that when we in the United States learned that fact, the direction of homebrewing turned.

By 1983, the concept of using fresh hops had been introduced, and Al Andrews introduced us to his tapper system for the Cornelius tank. That year we held the first Great American Beer Festival. Also, I was invited by the Master Brewers Association of the Americas (MBAA) to St. Louis to speak about homebrewing. Anheuser-Busch invited me to make two barrels of beer that would then be canned in St. Louis. I got a yeast culture from Coors and brewed two barrels of beer, a bock and a Scotch ale. When the beer was ready, an Anheuser-Busch truck came to my house and carted the beer to St. Louis, and my beer was canned in the middle of the night. The label had the logos of the MBAA, the AHA, and the American Society of Brewing Chemists. I think they were quite surprised at the quality of homebrewing.

During the years between 1983 and 1985, homebrew competitions grew from two hundred entries to four hundred. *zymurgy* came out on a regular basis, and we began to receive technical articles on beer spoilage organisms, closed fermentation, yeast culturing, homebrewed weizen beers, and quick beer that could be brewed and consumed within ten or fifteen days. Mathematical formulas pertaining to beer began to appear in the magazine. People who wrote for *zymurgy* then were Phil Moehler, Dave Logsdon, Gary Bauer, Dewayne Lee Saxton, Donald Thompson, Russ Schehrer, and many others who were homebrewers at that time and who are now brewmasters in their own microbreweries.

We also received international mail from homebrewers in other countries. After I wrote *Complete Joy of Homebrewing*, I spent my royalties on a trip to New Zealand, and my main contact there was a homebrew club that had contacted *zymurgy* four years earlier. Those homebrewers took me to the Lion Brewery in New Zealand where beer is delivered in tanks. Later, in a liquor store, I reached for a bottle of mead and read that it was made by Leon Havill in Rangiora, New Zealand. Right then and there, I called Rangiora and asked if I could visit the meadery. I flew down that day and met Leon and his mead for the first time. Now Leon and his wife Gay are here at this conference.

I told you about the beginnings of Beer and Steer. Well, it continued to be held in the mountains until we decided that our tenth year would be our last. We had had many great times, but we were getting older and had families and we decided to discontinue Beer and Steer. But we wanted to go out with a bang and hold the last one in the South Pacific. About sixty of us brewed up 100 gallons of beer, put it in twenty-five gallons tanks, packed it in boxes, and took it through customs in the Fiji Islands. We had a great ten days together. Beer and Steer Forever!

In 1987, the homebrewing community was talking about beer styles and differentiating between an Oktoberfest and a Pale Ale. This was the year that beer styles we had been brewing at home for years began to proliferate in the United States commercial market. Beers such as Weizen-Barley Wine, Porter, Stout, Bock, Pale Ale, and Celebration beers. We homebrewers began brewing those beers, and now you can find them available in liquor stores and taverns and even the large breweries are considering brewing these beers that we were pioneering ten years ago.

In looking ahead to the next ten years, let's keep beer and brewing and our lives in perspective and venture out into the jungle of other worlds. Let's take along a homebrew, and remember to "Relax and Don't Worry." Remember that when you travel, you don't know who you will meet in faraway lands and strange places making beer. As a fellow homebrewer, you can tell them, "I brew the beer I drink."

While Charlie Papazian reminisced about the American Homebrewers Association's ten grand years, the Pieds of June were anticipating a long-awaited event of their own. After Charlie was "roasted" by Michael Jackson, Fred Eckhardt, and Charlie Matsen, the Pie Terrorist gave him his "just desserts."

Charlie Papazian is the publisher of zymurgy, *president of American Hombrewers Association, and the designer of dozens of noted beer recipes.*

Relax. Don't Worry.

2.
Sensory Evaluation for Brewers

Jean-Xavier Guinard and Ian Robertson
Department of Food Science and Technology
University of California, Davis

Sensory evaluation is now recognized as a scientific discipline and has found extensive use in the brewing industry. Its applications include quality assurance, product development, and correlation with chemical, physical, and instrumental measures. In this paper, we will show how sensory evaluation techniques can be used by brewers. We will also show how homebrewers can benefit from sensory evaluation and turn their homebrew club into a valuable sensory panel.

Sensory Evaluation as a Research Tool

Sensory evaluation can be used as a research tool by university researchers, brewing companies, microbrewers, and homebrewers. Its purpose usually is to study the effect of one or several variables on the quality of beer. The development of the proper experimental

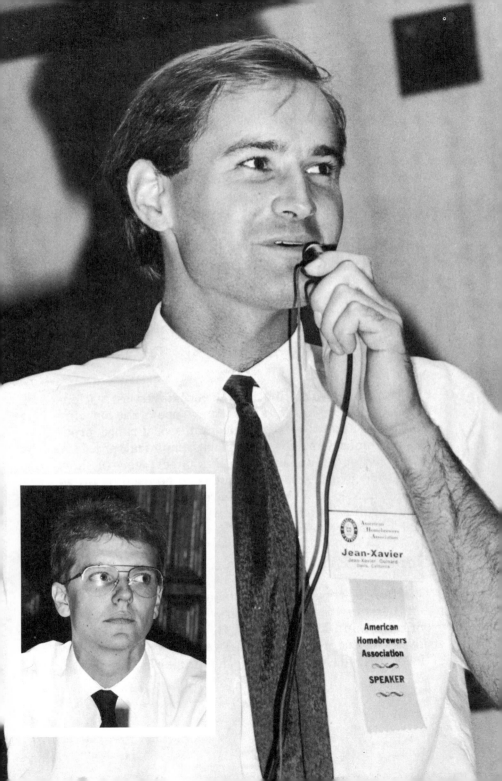

design, the choice of the appropriate sensory test(s), and the use of the right statistical procedures to analyze the data make a very powerful combination. However, even a small failure at any of these three stages of the research process can have disastrous consequences. It can lead to the mass production of a new product that will not serve its intended purpose, or to a costly and worthless investment to modify the brewing process. One should therefore exercise caution in conducting sensory research and be familiar with sensory evaluation procedures.

Unlike most chemical, physical, and instrumental measurements, sensory evaluation does not require expensive materials and sophisticated equipment. This makes it a valuable tool for the homebrewer. Furthermore, a homebrew club provides a set of motivated and experienced judges, the perfect panel for sensory evaluation experiments.

The Notion of Experimental Design

When a homebrewer wants to study the effect of one variable on beer quality, he or she should keep all variables but the one under study constant. For example, to study the effect of dry hopping with different hop varieties on beer flavor, one should prepare a single batch of wort, pitch it with yeast, split it into several lots, and then add one variety of hops to each fermentation vessel. The fermentation time and temperature, conditioning, and bottling practices should be the same for all beers. Only then can the homebrewer say that differences in beer flavor are caused by the hop variety used for dry hopping. The same rule applies for studying any other ingredient's effect on beer quality; i.e., never change more than one ingredient at a time and use the same brewing procedures for all beers.

The Choice of the Proper Sensory Test(s)

Research objectives have to be well defined. There are many different types of sensory tests that serve different purposes. The main distinction is between analytical-laboratory tests and consumer tests (Table 1). Analytical tests establish if there are differences among the experimental beers and define the nature and magnitude of these differences. Consumer tests determine acceptance, degree of liking, and preference. These are quite different objectives.

Analytical Tests

Usually, the first step is to determine if the samples, e.g., the beers dry-hopped with different varieties, are different. To answer that question, one can use a variety of discriminative tests, called difference tests. If the nature of the difference among beers is not specified, a duo-trio or a triangle test is used. In the duo-trio test, one sample (the reference) is presented first, followed by two samples one of which is identical to the reference. The judge is asked to find the one identical to the reference. In the triangle test, three samples are simultaneously presented in random order, two of which are identical. The judge is asked to identify the odd sample. When the difference among the beers can be specified, as in "Which beer is more floral?", one should use a pair-test or paired comparison in this method, two samples are presented simultaneously and the judge is asked to identify the

Table 1.
Types of Sensory Tests

I. Analytical Laboratory Tests

A. Discriminative	B. Quantitative	C. Qualitative
1. Difference tests	1. Scaling	1. Descriptive analysis
a. Paired comparison	a. Category	a. Flavor profile
b. Duo-trio	b. Ratio	b. Quantitative descriptive analysis
c. Triangle		c. Deviation from reference
	2. Ranking	
	3. Duration	
	a. Time Intensity	

II. Affective Consumer Tests

A. Acceptance	B. Preference	C. Hedonic
1. Accept/reject	1. Select one over another option	1. Degree of like/dislike

sample with the greater intensity of the specified characteristic. Difference tests should always be conducted using trained, experienced judges. These methods can reliably determine quite small and subtle differences among beers.

Once it has been shown that samples are different, the second step is to define the magnitude of the difference. For this, we use a quantitative procedure such as a scaling method. The intensity of a specified attribute is scored by assigning it a rating on a category or a ratio scale. This allows differences among beers to be reported as numbers. A category scale can be a numerical scale ("score the intensity of bitterness on a scale from 0 to 10, where 0 is none and 10 is extreme bitterness") or a graphic scale (a line anchored with the words "none" and "extreme" or "low" and "high" on which the judge marks the intensity of the rated attribute). When a ratio scale is used, the judge is asked to determine how much higher or lower the intensity of an attribute is compared to a reference. Like difference tests, scaling requires trained judges.

Alternatively, ranking tests can be used when many samples are to be compared. These require judges to arrange a series of samples in an ascending or descending order of intensity for a given attribute. Whereas ranking is simple and can be done by relatively inexperienced judges, it does not determine the magnitude of the differences among samples.

Another technique called time-intensity has found extensive use in sensory research. It quantifies the temporal changes in sensation that occur from the time beer is placed in the mouth until extinction of the sensation. The judge moves a stick along a slot labelled "none" to "extreme." The stick is interfaced to a microcomputer that records intensity vs. time. Using this technique, we have studied the effect of repeated beer ingestion on temporal perception of bitterness (Guinard et al., 1986). It is, however, a method ill suited for homebrew clubs because it requires expensive hardware and software.

The third step defines the nature of the differences among samples. It is qualitative. Descriptive analysis or "flavor profiling" are the most commonly used techniques. They are based on the fact that a person can be trained to consistently and reproducibly rate the intensities of those attributes that make up the profile under study. A panel of judges trained for flavor profiling is a great asset for a large brewing company as well as for a homebrew club. It can be considered as a very reliable instrument and may have a higher sensitivity than most gas chromatographs. For example, the human nose can detect sulfur compounds such as ethanethiol or diethyl sulfide in beer at concentrations as low as one part per billion (1 microgram per liter).

Consumer Tests

A word about so-called "consumer" tests. They are affective tests. Their purpose is to determine acceptance, preference, and/or degree of liking of a product. They have no analytical value. They are administered using people representative of the target population, i.e., the ultimate users of the product, not trained judges. Such tests include the paired preference test in which two samples are presented to a judge who reports which one he or she prefers. Alternatively, a judge may receive several

samples and be asked to rank them according to preference. Another popular method is the hedonic method in
which the judge marks his opinion of a product on a 9-point
hedonic scale where 0 is "dislike extremely" and 9 is "like
extremely." This method is traditionally used to determine a sample's degree of liking.

The most frequent mistake found in the brewing
literature is the use of consumer tests when analytical
tests should be used, or vice versa. Assessing the effect of
the yeast strain on beer quality by asking consumers (or
untrained panelists) which one they prefer is wrong.
Difference tests and descriptive analysis by trained
judges should be used in that case. Confounding hedonic
terms with intensity and/or quality terms also is errone-
ous. For example, "ideal or objectionable bitterness"
(hedonic or subjective terms) is not a substitute for "low or
high bitterness" (intensity terms) in qualitative sensory
evaluation. Fortunately, the pioneering work of Meilgaard, Pangborn, Clapperton, Mecredy, Neilson, and
others has given an edge in sensory evaluation to the
brewing industry and the literature is now virtually error-
free.

Statistics: Friend or Foe?

Statistics combine with sensory evaluation to
make a powerful research tool. They allow the researcher
to determine the significance of the results by discriminat-
ing between actual differences and random error. Generally, for each type of sensory test there is a corresponding
statistical test. Tables are available to determine the
significance of the results of paired, duo-trio, and triangle
tests give the minimum number of correct judgments to

establish significance at various probability levels for different tests (Tables 2, 3, and 4).

The probability to give the right answer by chance alone is one-half for a pair-test or a duo-trio and one-third for a triangle test. A one-tailed test is used when there is only one correct answer, e.g., when the judges are asked to determine which sample is more floral. A two-tailed test applies when there is no intuitively correct answer, e.g., when the judges are asked which sample they prefer. If we want to determine whether a beer dry-hopped with Saaz is more floral than one dry-hopped with Chinook, we can have twenty judges in our homebrew club perform a paired comparison.

Checking Table 2, which gives the minimum number of correct judgments to establish significance at the five percent level (traditionally the minimum acceptable level) for a one-tailed test, we find that fifteen out of twenty judges must select the same sample for the difference to be significant. If only fourteen judges select the Chinook sample, we cannot conclude that it is more floral than the Saaz sample. If we want to determine which beer would be liked better by beer drinkers, we can ask a sample of fifty consumers in a bar which beer they prefer.

Table 3 (two-tailed test) indicates that at least thirty-three out of fifty judges must indicate the same preference (Saaz or Chinook) to conclude that one beer is significantly preferred over the other.

To interpret the results of a ranking test, we can consult Table 5, which gives the difference between sums of ranks required for significance at the 5 percent level. For example, if a panel of ten judges ranks five beers for

Beer and Brewing Vol.8

Table 2   Minimum Numbers of Correct Judgments to Establish Significance at Various Probability Levels for Paired-Comparison and Duo-Trio Tests (one-tailed, $p = \frac{1}{2}$)[a]

No. of trials (n)	Probability levels						
	0.05	0.04	0.03	0.02	0.01	0.005	0.001
7	7	7	7	7	7		
8	7	7	8	8	8	8	
9	8	8	8	8	9	9	
10	9	9	9	9	10	10	10
11	9	9	10	10	10	11	11
12	10	10	10	10	11	11	12
13	10	11	11	11	12	12	13
14	11	11	11	12	12	13	13
15	12	12	12	12	13	13	14
16	12	12	13	13	14	14	15
17	13	13	13	14	14	15	16
18	13	14	14	14	15	15	16
19	14	14	15	15	15	16	17
20	15	15	15	16	16	17	18
21	15	15	16	16	17	17	18
22	16	16	16	17	17	18	19
23	16	17	17	17	18	19	20
24	17	17	18	18	19	19	20
25	18	18	18	19	19	20	21
26	18	18	19	19	20	20	22
27	19	19	19	20	20	21	22
28	19	20	20	20	21	22	23
29	20	20	21	21	22	22	24
30	20	21	21	22	22	23	24
31	21	21	22	22	23	24	25
32	22	22	22	23	24	24	26
33	22	23	23	23	24	25	26
34	23	23	23	24	25	25	27
35	23	24	24	25	25	26	27
36	24	24	25	25	26	27	28
37	24	25	25	26	26	27	29
38	25	25	26	26	27	28	29
39	26	26	26	27	28	28	30
40	26	27	27	27	28	29	30
41	27	27	27	28	29	30	31
42	27	28	28	29	29	30	32
43	28	28	29	29	30	31	32
44	28	29	29	30	31	31	33
45	29	29	30	30	31	32	34
46	30	30	30	31	32	33	34
47	30	30	31	31	32	33	35
48	31	31	31	32	33	34	36
49	31	32	32	33	34	34	36
50	32	32	33	33	34	35	37
60	37	38	38	39	40	41	43
70	43	43	44	45	46	47	49
80	48	49	49	50	51	52	55
90	54	54	55	56	57	58	61
100	59	60	60	61	63	64	66

[a] Values (X) not appearing in table may be derived from:
$$X = (z \sqrt{n} + n + 1)/2.$$

Source: E. B. Roessler et al., *Journal of Food Science*, 1978, *43*, 940-947. Copyright © by Institute of Food Technologists. Reprinted with permission of author and publisher.

Table 3   Minimum Numbers of Agreeing Judgments
Necessary to Establish Significance at Various Probability
Levels for the Paired-Preference Tests (two-tailed, p = ½)[a]

No. of trials (n)	Probability levels						
	0.05	0.04	0.03	0.02	0.01	0.005	0.001
7	7	7	7	7			
8	8	8	8	8	8		
9	8	8	9	9	9	9	
10	9	9	9	10	10	10	
11	10	10	10	10	11	11	11
12	10	10	11	11	11	12	12
13	11	11	11	12	12	12	13
14	12	12	12	12	13	13	14
15	12	12	13	13	13	14	14
16	13	13	13	14	14	14	15
17	13	14	14	14	15	15	16
18	14	14	15	15	15	16	17
19	15	15	15	15	16	16	17
20	15	16	16	16	17	17	18
21	16	16	16	17	17	18	19
22	17	17	17	17	18	18	19
23	17	17	18	18	19	19	20
24	18	18	18	19	19	20	21
25	18	19	19	19	20	20	21
26	19	19	19	20	20	21	22
27	20	20	20	20	21	22	23
28	20	20	21	21	22	22	23
29	21	21	21	22	22	23	24
30	21	22	22	22	23	24	25
31	22	22	22	23	24	24	25
32	23	23	23	23	24	25	26
33	23	23	24	24	25	25	27
34	24	24	24	25	25	26	27
35	24	25	25	25	26	27	28
36	25	25	25	26	27	27	29
37	25	26	26	26	27	28	29
38	26	26	27	27	28	29	30
39	27	27	27	28	28	29	31
40	27	27	28	28	29	30	31
41	28	28	28	29	30	30	32
42	28	29	29	29	30	31	32
43	29	29	30	30	31	32	33
44	29	30	30	30	31	32	34
45	30	30	31	31	32	33	34
46	31	31	31	32	33	33	35
47	31	31	32	32	33	34	36
48	32	32	32	33	34	35	36
49	32	33	33	34	34	35	37
50	33	33	34	34	35	36	37
60	39	39	39	40	41	42	44
70	44	45	45	46	47	48	50
80	50	50	51	51	52	53	56
90	55	56	56	57	58	59	61
100	61	61	62	63	64	65	67

Beer and Brewing Vol.8

Table 4   Minimum Numbers of Correct Judgments to Establish Significance at Various Probability Levels for the Triangle Tests (one tailed, p = 1/3)[b]

No. of trials (n)	Probability levels						
	0.05	0.04	0.03	0.02	0.01	0.005	0.001
5	4	5	5	5	5	5	
6	5	5	5	5	6	6	
7	5	6	6	6	6	7	7
8	6	6	6	6	7	7	8
9	6	7	7	7	7	8	8
10	7	7	7	7	8	8	9
11	7	7	8	8	8	9	10
12	8	8	8	8	9	9	10
13	8	8	9	9	9	10	11
14	9	9	9	9	10	10	11
15	9	9	10	10	10	11	12
16	9	10	10	10	11	11	12
17	10	10	10	11	11	12	13
18	10	11	11	11	12	12	13
19	11	11	11	12	12	13	14
20	11	11	12	12	13	13	14
21	12	12	12	13	13	14	15
22	12	12	13	13	14	14	15
23	12	13	13	13	14	15	16
24	13	13	13	14	15	15	16
25	13	14	14	14	15	16	17
26	14	14	14	15	15	16	17
27	14	14	15	15	16	17	18
28	15	15	15	16	16	17	18
29	15	15	16	16	17	17	19
30	15	16	16	16	17	18	19
31	16	16	16	17	18	18	20
32	16	16	17	17	18	19	20
33	17	17	17	18	18	19	21
34	17	17	18	18	19	20	21
35	17	18	18	19	19	20	22
36	18	18	18	19	20	20	22
37	18	18	19	19	20	21	22
38	19	19	19	20	21	21	23
39	19	19	20	20	21	22	23
40	19	20	20	21	21	22	24
41	20	20	20	21	22	23	24
42	20	20	21	21	22	23	25
43	20	21	21	22	23	24	25
44	21	21	22	22	23	24	26
45	21	22	22	23	24	24	26
46	22	22	22	23	24	25	27
47	22	22	23	23	24	25	27
48	22	23	23	24	25	26	27
49	23	23	24	24	25	26	28
50	23	24	24	25	26	26	28
60	27	27	28	29	30	31	33
70	31	31	32	33	34	35	37
80	35	35	36	36	38	39	41
90	38	39	40	40	42	43	45
100	42	43	43	44	45	47	49

[b] Values (X) not appearing in table may be derived from:

$$X = 0.4714 \, z\sqrt{n} + [(2n + 3)/6].$$

Table 5.
Difference Between Sums of Ranks*
Required for Significance at the 5% Level
(Hollander and Wolfe, 1973)

Number of judges	Number of samples							
	3	4	5	6	7	8	9	10
3	6	8	10	13	15	18	20	22
4	7	10	12	15	18	21	24	26
5	8	11	14	17	20	23	27	30
6	9	12	15	19	22	26	29	33
7	9	13	16	20	24	28	32	36
8	10	14	18	22	26	30	34	38
9	10	15	19	23	27	32	36	41
10	11	15	20	24	29	34	38	43
11	11	16	21	26	30	35	40	45
12	12	17	21	27	32	37	42	48
13	12	18	23	28	33	39	44	50
14	13	18	24	29	34	40	46	52
15	13	19	24	30	36	42	47	53

*Add up the ranks obtained by each beer. Then compare the difference between the sum of ranks of two beers to the value shown in the table. If the difference is higher, the two beers are significantly different.

bitterness intensity, two beers will differ significantly in bitterness intensity if the difference between their sum of ranks is higher than twenty.

Misapplication of probability tables for determining significance in paired, duo-trio, and triangle tests are examples of common misuse of statistical procedures in sensory evaluation. The most common mistake is to use a one-tailed test when a two-tailed test should be used or vice versa.

More advanced statistics (analysis of variance, multivariate statistics) are used when a lot of data are collected. They require software that is not readily available to homebrewers. Imagine that the flavor profile (ten attributes) of beers fermented with twenty different yeast strains is determined in duplicate by a trained panel of fifteen judges. This generates six thousand numbers. A type of multivariate analysis called factor analysis is used to boil the information contained in the data down to the main relations among the yeast strains. Factor analysis generates a space in which yeast strains are clustered based on their flavor characteristics in much the same way that a map of the U.S. would be generated if one fed the distances among American cities to the same computer program. Statistics: friend or foe? Definitely friend, as long as you keep up with them.

Sensory Evaluation as a Quality Control and Trouble-shooting Tool

Flavor profiling and off-flavor detection are two sensory evaluation techniques used to monitor beer quality on a routine basis and to detect sensory defects.

The production of a beer with a constant quality is the main concern of large breweries. Similarly, a home-brewer may want to be able to make the same product repeatedly. In both cases, the brewer must resort to using flavor profiling to define and then keep track of his product's flavor. Flavor profiling is a very powerful technique when properly used; a waste of time and energy otherwise. Extreme care must be exercised in (1) selecting the descriptors of the flavor attributes; and (2) training the panel. The descriptors used must have a universal meaning and carry no affective or hedonic value. Ideally, they should be translatable in any language. This means that no subjective descriptors such as balanced/unbalanced, good/bad, young/mature should be used. Such terms have different meanings for different people. Also, standards should be available that correspond to each descriptor. For example, a few microliters of diacetyl can be added to beer to make a standard for "buttery." Similarly, a bitterness standard can be prepared by spiking a beer with iso-alpha-acids (isomerized hop extract).

The panel, e.g., brewery employees or homebrew club members, must be trained to evaluate the attributes with consistency and reproducibility. Consistency is the measure of agreement among the judges; reproducibility is their ability to give the same ratings to the same beer on different occasions. Provided that one dedicated member is willing to prepare standards, a homebrew club can train to be a skilled panel in a few sessions. A standard scorecard can then be designed and adopted which will include between eight and fifteen sensory attributes. The attributes might be limited to flavor properties only or might also encompass appearance, aroma, flavor (aroma and taste), and tactile properties. Such a scorecard can be used for all the beers made by the brewery or homebrew club, or a specific scorecard can be designed for the different types of beers to be evaluated on a regular basis, i.e., one for ales, one for lagers, one for Lambics, etc. A very well-documented glossary of beer flavor descriptors is available in the *zymurgy* Special Issue 1987. The scorecard that we use at U.C. Davis for some applications is reproduced in Table 6.

Off-flavor detection is similar to flavor profiling except that it focuses on defective flavors. A panel trained to detect and recognize off-flavors using various standards is a valuable tool for troubleshooting. For example, standards can be prepared by spoiling wort or beer with pure cultures of various contaminants, e.g., Pediococcus, Brettanomyces, etc., or by spiking beer with various undesirable chemicals, e.g., H2S, dimethyl sulfide, diacetyl, guaiacol, etc. If the panel can consistently recognize these characters, the source of the off-flavor often can be identified and corrected faster than with more laborious instrumental methods of analysis.

The following conclusions should be drawn from this review of sensory procedures. Sensory evaluation techniques can provide valuable information if they are used in the right way. The distinction between analytical and consumer tests should be kept in mind. Not only large brewing companies but also microbreweries and homebrew clubs can successfully develop sensory evaluation programs. The applications for research, quality control, new product development, and troubleshooting are many.

A condensation of guidelines for the use of sensory procedures by a homebrew club is presented in Table 6.

Table 6.
U.C. Davis Scorecard for Descriptive Analysis
NAME _____

Please rate the intensity of the following parameters using a scale from 0 to 10 (0 = none; 10 = extreme).

Attribute Sample code				
Aroma				
Fruity				
Floral				
Oxidized				
Grassy				
Grainy				
Phenolic/medicinal				
Diacetyl/buttery				
Yeasty				
Sulfury				
Skunky/light-struck				
Taste				
Bitter				
Sour				
Sweet				
Metallic				
Texture				
Carbonation				
Astringency				

Table 7.
Sensory Evaluation for the Homebrew Club

Panel:
Homebrew club members. The number of judges depends on the nature of the test. At least fifteen are needed for difference tests and five for flavor profiling. Use judges of demonstrated ability.

Locale:
Well lighted room, free of extraneous odors, noise, and bright colors. Temperature around 70 degrees F.

Equipment:
Ideally, judges should be separated in order not to influence each other. Partitions can be placed on a large table to make booths. Use clean beer glasses. A recurved shape retains volatiles better. Samples are coded with three-digit numbers to minimize biases.

Time of day:
Avoid tasting right after meals. Less important than panel motivation.

Serving temperature:
Anywhere between 50 and 65 degrees F, depending on the type of beer to be evaluated. Avoid large (5 degrees F) variations in temperature among samples.

Number of samples:
For difference tests, keep number of pairs, duo-trios, or triangles below ten; fatigue might set in otherwise. Ranking gets difficult above six samples. For flavor profiling, five samples is a maximum, especially if the number of attributes to rate is high (ten or higher).

Training:

Perform difference, ranking, and scaling tests on commercial samples. For flavor profiling, prepare standards for each attribute. The panel should check them until it is very familiar with all of them. Do flavor profiles of commercial beers on several occasions. Check judges for consistency (agreement with rest of panel) and reproducibility. Train judges to recognize common off-flavors by preparing adequate samples.

Preparation of Reference Standards for Flavor Profiling

Joint working groups of the American Society of Brewing Chemists, the European Brewery Convention, and the Master Brewers Association of the Americas have developed a beer flavor terminology (Meilgaard et al., 1979) for use in flavor profiling. Based on this work, Noonan and Papazian (1988) have proposed guidelines for beer aroma recognition. Indeed, one of the basic principles of the system of flavor terminology is that the meaning of each term is illustrated with reference standards. Ideally, pure chemicals are used in the preparation of standards to ensure that each term is used in the exact same way by all users of the flavor wheel. It is reasonable to assume that pure chemicals do not vary too much in flavor around the world.

However, the preparation of standards with pure chemicals has several drawbacks for homebrewers: (1) pure chemicals can be expensive; (2) they are not always readily available; and (3) they may be difficult to handle (a fume hood and micropipettes are usually required). Furthermore, the standards suggested by Meilgaard et al.

Table 8.
Flavor Descriptors and Reference Standards

General descriptor	Specific descriptor	Reference standard[1]
Alcoholic	Alcohol	15 ml of 95% ethanol
Spicy	Clove	2 cloves
Floral	Geranium	Piece of geranium leaf
	Violet	Few crushed violet petals
	Rose	Few crushed rose petals
Hoppy	Hops	Few pellets of fresh hops (1 standard per variety)
Fruity	Lemon	10 ml juice and peel
	Grapefruit	10 ml juice and peel
	Orange	10 ml juice and peel
	Raspberry	4-5 crushed raspberries
	Black currant	15 ml Ribena® or cassis cream
	Cherry	15 ml brine of canned cherries
	Peach	30 ml peach nectar
	Apricot	25 ml apricot nectar
	Pear	30 ml pear nectar
	Melon	3 slices of fresh cantaloupe
	Apple	30 ml apple juice
	Banana	2 slices of banana

	Artificial fruit	1 tsp. Tropical punch Koolaid®
Winey	Wine	50 ml of jug white wine
Vegetative	Grassy	Freshly-cut grass (no beer)
	Hay/Straw	Finely-cut pieces of hay-straw (no beer)
	Tea	5-10 flakes of black tea
	Tobacco	5-10 flakes of tobacco
Cooked vegetable	Green beans	15 ml brine from canned green beans
	Asparagus	10 ml brine from canned asparagus
Grainy	Malt	Handul of kernels
	Barley	or 2 tablespoons
	Wheat	of mashed grain in
	Rice	a glass (no beer)
	Corn	
Worty	Wort	1:1 wort/beer
Caramel	Honey	3 tablespoons of honey
	Butterscotch	2 cut Kraft® caramels
	Buttery	Few drops of imitation butter flavored extract
	Licorice	Few pieces of licorice twists
	Soy	3 ml of soy sauce
	Chocolate	Few drops of chocolate

		flavored extract or 2 tsp powdered cocoa
	Molasses	1 tsp molasses
	Coffee	1/2 tsp ground coffee
Nutty	Walnut	10 crushed walnuts
	Almond	Few drops of almond extract
Pungent	Ethyl acetate	Few drops of nail polish remover
	Acetic acid	15 ml white vinegar
Sulfury	H2S	Yolk of hard-boiled egg (no beer)
	Cabbage	10 ml brine from boiled cabbage leaves
	Sweet corn	15 ml brine from canned corn
	Burnt match	Tips of 3 burnt wooden matches
	Rubber	2 small pieces of rubber tubing
	Lightstruck	Leave clear bottle in sun
Yeasty	Yeast	Few mls of fresh yeast slurry
Oxidized	Oxidized	Incubate beer at 100° F for a few hours
Soapy	Soap	Few flakes of Ivory® soap

Earthy	Mushroom	2 chopped up mushrooms
	Moldy	Slice of moldy bread (no beer)
Papery	Cardboard	Few cardboard pieces
Petroleum	Plastic	Few pieces of cut up plastic tubing
	Tar	Few drops of roofing tar
	Gasoline	2-3 drops of gasoline
Burnt	Smoky	2-3 drops of smoky flavor extract
	Burnt toast	Few pieces of burnt toast
Medicinal	Phenolic	0.1 ml guaiacol
Lactic	Lactic	10 ml brine from canned sauerkraut
Cheesy	Cheese	Few crumbles of Feta cheese
Meaty	Meaty	10 ml beef broth
Fishy	Shrimp	3 ml shrimp brine
Sweet	Sugar	5 g sucrose
Sour	Acid	5 g citric acid

Salty	Salt	1 g sodium chloride
Bitter	Iso-alpha-acids	Few drops of isomerized hop extract
Astringent	Tannins	3 g of alun or grape seed tannin
Viscous	Viscous	1 tablespoon of Polycose®
Body	Body	15 g of dextrins

[1] In 12 oz. beer unless otherwise specified.

(1982) are prepared using a single pure chemical in a base beer. A significant problem with this approach is the inability of a single compound to faithfully reproduce a complex aroma characteristic, such as grassy or floral.

Consequently, based on our routine use of flavor profiling for research or teaching, we suggest the use of foodstuffs or raw materials readily available throughout the world during most seasons for the preparation of reference standards Note that the list of terms differs slightly from the original list given by Meilgaard (1979).

A twelve-ounce bottle of neutral beer (commercial light beer in long-neck bottles) is used for the preparation of most standards. Open the bottle, spike with the appropriate material, recap, and incubate for at least a few hours before use (ideally overnight) at cool temperature (50 degrees F). Once the standards have been poured, it is best to cover the glasses with a Petri dish to retain volatiles better.

As mentioned by Noble et al. (1987), the intensity of a reference standard will vary with its function. To define a specific term, an intensity that provides a very obvious aroma is recommended. On the other hand, to train judges for flavor profiling, lower intensities are needed to better illustrate that aroma characteristic at the level at which it may be found in beer. Also, it is often appropriate to combine terms to describe a particular flavor characteristic (for example, rose/violet as a floral term, or peach/apricot as a fruity term). In such a case, a dual standard is prepared.

References

Guinard, J.-X.; R.M. Pangborn; and M.J. Lewis (1986). "Effect of repeated ingestion on temporal perception of bitterness in beer." J. Am. Soc. Brew. Chem. 44:28-32.

Hollander, M., and D.A. Wolfe, "Nonparametric Statistical Methods," Wiley, New York; 1973.

Meilgaard, M.C.; C.E. Dalgliesh; and J.F. Clapperton (1979). "Beer flavor terminology." J. Am. Soc. Brew. Chem. 37:47-52.

Meilgaard, M.C.; D.S. Reid; and K.A. Wuborski (1982). "Reference standards for beer flavor terminology system." J. Am. Soc. Brew. Chem. 40:119-128.

Noble, A.C.; R.A. Arnold; J. Buechsenstein; E.J. Leach; J.O. Schmidt, and P.M. Stern (1987). "Modification of a standardized system of wine aroma terminology." Am. J. Enol. Vitic. 38:143-146.

Noonan, G., and C. Papazian (1988). "Aroma ID kit development. Tenth Annual Conference on Quality Beer and Brewing." Denver, CO.

Jean-Xavier Guinard and Ian Robertson are Brewing Science graduate students at the University of California-Davis and have worked with Dr. Michael Lewis.

Brewmaster Fred Scheer judging
the Professional Panel Tasting at GABF

3.
Issues in All-Grain Brewing

Dave Miller
Author and 1981 Homebrewer of the Year

I am going to talk about techniques, but before I do that, I want to make one point regarding materials. A friend of mine has bought three different samples of so-called Munich malt from three different suppliers in the last year. One made a pale beer, the second an amber beer, and the third a dark beer. The moral of the story is that we need specifications for our malts—not only color, but also extract, nitrogen content, diastatic power, and so on. Up until a few years ago, homebrewers were working blindfolded in setting hop rates. Fortunately, that is no longer the case, but we are still in the dark when it comes to our most fundamental ingredient.

I have a couple of suggestions. To my fellow homebrewers: start bugging your suppliers for specifications on the malt you buy. To those suppliers, whether wholesalers or retailers: please get us some data! The malting companies have it; it's up to you to ask for it.

With that out of the way, let's get on to the main topic. If there is one point I want to make, it is that amateurs have to be pragmatic. We work on a small scale with limited and often primitive equipment. We cannot always follow commercial brewing practice, especially in our mashing and sparging techniques. We have to be prepared to experiment and adapt.

Over the past few years I have been asked to help sort out problems that my friends were having with their mashes. I have learned two things from these consultations: first, the difficulties I experienced when I was getting started are fairly common; second, the solutions I arrived at will work as well for other brewers as they did for me.

Nonetheless, a pragmatist like myself would have to say that the only test that matters is your results. If your system satisfies you and your beer is good, don't change a thing. But if you feel there is still room for improvement in your operation, you might want to try some of the techniques I have adopted.

Many of our difficulties can be traced back to the very first step of the process: crushing the malt. Our old friend the Corona grain mill is an adequate tool—certainly better than a blender or coffee grinder—but it is far from ideal. Let me quote you de Clerck's specifications for an acceptable crush: husks, 20 to 25 percent; flour, 30 to 40 percent; grits, 30 to 40 percent. It is also specified that the husks remain intact, and that there be three times more fine than coarse grits.

I have been unable to analyze my crushed malt the way the breweries do, with a multigrade sifter, but you can see just by looking at it that the malt you run through your

Corona is nowhere near this standard. If you adjusted it right, many husks remain intact, but others have been chopped into pieces or even powdered. Even more significant, coarse grits form the largest part of the crush. This is unavoidable because the grinding plates must be set to a wide gap in order to avoid pulverizing the husks.

The crush of the malt has important consequences, but before I go on to discuss them, I want to consider an obvious question: why not replace the Corona mill with something better? Well, this is easier said than done. The ideal tool for crushing malt is a commercial mill with two or three pairs of rollers. Unfortunately, the design cannot be scaled down. The rollers must be ten inches in diameter and machined to fairly exacting specifications. Even a simple mill with a single pair of rollers is a bulky apparatus that cannot be manufactured and sold at a price most homebrewers could afford. Most of us are stuck with the basic screw-feed, single-rotating-plate design of the Corona.

The two complaints I hear from beginning grain brewers are first, low extract; and second, slow and difficult sparging. Both of these problems are usually caused by the imperfect crush of the malt. Let's look at extract first.

There are three steps involved in the conversion of malt starch to sugar: gelatinization, liquefaction, and saccharification. The first step is probably the least understood by homebrewers. In the barley grain, starch is contained in tiny granules within the cells of the endosperm, which is the storage compartment of the kernel. During malting, the cell walls are broken down by cytase enzymes. This is why well modified malt is "mealy" (soft and friable) while raw barley grains are "steely" and hard to chew. However, the starch granules themselves are for the most part unaffected by the malting process.

When a slurry of starch granules is heated to a certain temperature (149 degrees F. in the case of barley starch), the granules break apart and the individual molecules of starch disperse in the liquid, forming a viscous suspension. If you have ever used cornstarch or flour to thicken a sauce, you have observed this phenomenon, which is known as gelatinization. This is a vital step in mashing because until the starch molecules are suspended in water, they cannot be attacked by the malt enzymes.

No doubt you have observed that your mash does not thicken like gravy as it is raised to starch conversion temperature. The reason is that the second step, liquefaction, follows immediately upon the first. As soon as the starch molecules are released, they are attacked by the liquefying enzyme, alpha amylase. When the starch molecule is broken into chains small enough to be soluble in water, it is said to have been liquefied. In a normal mash, this happens so fast that at any given moment there is relatively little gelatinized starch in suspension. It passes rapidly from the ungelatinized to the liquefied state.

The final step of the process is saccharification, in which alpha and beta amylase work together to reduce the liquefied starch to a mixture of sugars and limit dextrins. This is of course the whole object of mashing, but for our purposes today is not important. The problems come in the first step.

In a well-crushed malt, the vast majority of the endosperms have been ground into flour or fine grits.

Obviously, the smaller the bits of starchy material are, the more readily they will absorb water and the quicker the starch granules they contain will become gelatinized. On the other hand, imperfectly crushed malt like ours will take longer to yield its full extract.

Note also that iodine only tests for liquefied starch. It gives no indication of how much starch is still locked up, ungelatinized, in the coarse-grits fraction of the malt. This is why it is a mistake to rely on the iodine test. It will often indicate that saccharification is complete in twenty to thirty minutes; but if mashing is stopped at this point, a considerable amount of starch will never reach the gelatinization stage. The result: low extract.

I recommend a rest of one to two hours for starch conversion. I have gotten excellent extraction rates following the staggered schedule in Table 1. It also allows you to control fermentability. To avoid the tedious job of temperature control, I built an insulated box that will hold the mash within the specified range for the required time. I simply raise the mash to the starting value and set the kettle in the box for the duration of the rest. With most mashes, the only further attention required is a brief stirring at the halfway point. These figures are what I get with my equipment and only with the kind of mash that's described behind the asterisks. It's an all-pale malt mash. You can get an apparent attenuation rate of up to 80 percent with a two-hour mash.

However, even if you prolong mashing to get complete conversion, you can still experience low extracts due to your sparging process. Once again, the "gritty" nature of our crushed malt is at the root of the problem. At the end of mashing, the grits are soft and porous, like tiny sponges.

Table 1
Mash Schedules

Protein rest:
30 min. @ 132 - 130 F (most beers)
45 min. @ 123 - 121 F (wheat beers, recipes with flaked barley)

Starch conv. rest:

	apparent attenuation*	Terminal gravity*
120 min. @ 150 - 141 F**	80%	10
90 min. @ 153 - 145 F	75%	13
60 min. @ 155 - 150 F	68%	16
60 min. @ 158 - 153 F	60%	20

* Approximate figures for a grist of 100% American 2-row or 6-row lager malt. Terminal gravity figures assume an Original Gravity of 50, and attenuative yeast.

** With adjuncts mashes or low-enzyme malts (e.g. Munich malt, wheat malt, British malts) boost temp. back to 150 F at halfway point.

And true to their nature, they hold a considerable amount of heavy, viscous sweet wort. Getting it out is not easy.

The only way I have found to get the full brewing value from my malt is to sparge with a large volume of water—normally, five gallons for a five-gallon batch of beer. This is sufficient to give an extract that is within a point or two of the theoretical maximum. However, intensive sparging is not foolproof, and you have to watch out for the pitfalls.

First of all, the large volume of sparge water will do no good unless the filter bed is established and all cloudy wort is recirculated before sparging begins. Theoretically the reasoning is obvious, but neophyte mashers tend to be impatient and may be tempted to start adding sparge water as soon as the outflow from the lauter tun begins to slow down.

Second, to avoid collecting too much wort (more than can be boiled down to four and a half gallons or so in an hour and a half half to two hours), you will have to compensate for your large volume of sparge water by cutting down the volume of mash water. I use about one and one-third quarts per pound of barley malt, and only one quart per pound of flakes or wheat malt. A thick mash has other benefits as well—most importantly, it increases the survival time for the malt enzymes. This makes it a natural complement to a long mash.

Third, there are well-documented problems with oversparging. As the mash is rinsed, its buffering system is diluted and the pH tends to rise to that of the sparge water. When this happens, large quantities of tannins are leached from the husks. My way around this is to lower the pH of my sparge water to 5.7 with a small quantity of lactic acid. It may be unorthodox, but it works: before I adopted this measure, my last runnings would have the color and flavor of weak tea. Now they are almost clear and have no astringency at all.

I might add that there is another danger that is not directly related to the volume of sparge water, but is worth thinking about. In any mash, a small percentage of the starch will not be gelatinized. If the sparge water temperature is too high—over 168 degrees F—this starch can be released from the grits and end up in your boiler. One of my friends found that, even though his mash would test negative for starch, his wort would test positive after sparging. He solved the problem by lowering the temperature of his sparge water. I recommend sparging at between 165 and 168 degrees F, but 160 degrees is better than 170 degrees.

Now we come to the second problem faced by amateurs, which is a difficult runoff and sparge. I have already indicated that this is caused in large part to the crush of the malt, but the design of the lauter tun also plays a part. Over the course of several years I arrived at a lauter tun design which I find fairly satisfactory. It gives a total runoff/recirculation/sparging time of one to two hours, depending on the composition of the mash. The minimum time is for a grist consisting entirely of six-row malt; the maximum is for a weizenbier recipe using two-thirds finely crushed wheat malt. These times are not as quick as I would prefer, but I have never been able to improve upon them without reducing my extract.

My lauter tun is based on a grain bag strainer, similar to those pictured in Dave Line's books. The bag is held in a six-gallon plastic trash can. My only contribution to the design is the false bottom, which is the sawed-off portion of a regular five-gallon plastic food-grade pail drilled with quarter-inch holes on half-inch centers. The mesh bottom of the grain bag is a very coarse weave, and straining action is minimal. Until the filter bed is established, lots of draff washes through. Nonetheless, the system is quicker to operate than any other I have tried, and produces very clean wort.

By way of comparison, last year I built a conventional homebrewer's lauter tun consisting of two plastic buckets. The inner bucket is drilled with eighth-inch holes on quarter-inch centers. The best sparge times I have been able to get are about half again as long as my own setup. When I dump out the spent grains, I find that at least 30 percent of the holes are plugged with grits. I believe that this largely explains the time differential.

With both lauter tuns, I have experimented with different procedures. For example, I have tried the tactic of running off the sweet wort very slowly in order to avoid packing the filter bed. This gives a slightly looser bed, but it doubles or triples the time required for the runoff/recirculation phase. It might save five or ten minutes with the sparge, but at the price of one-half to one hour in the earlier steps. With a coarse strainer, it also results in repeated blockages of the tap. The whole procedure is frustrating as well as time-consuming.

I have also compared underletting with leaving the space between the false and true bottoms empty. With both tuns, I have found that underletting increases the runoff/recirculation time, because it increases the volume of wort that must be collected before the filter bed establishes itself. Sparge time is about equal, which means that

In celebration of ten years of glorious homebrewing, past Homebrewers of the Year were honored. The Stars of Homebrew included (from left) Ray Spangler, 1987; Byron Burch, 1986; Russ Schehrer, 1985; Dewayne Lee Saxton, 1984; Nancy Vineyard, 1983; and Dave Miller, 1981.

the bed is packed to about the same degree in both cases. Efficiency is diminished because some of the sparge water is used for underletting.

Another experiment I have tried is omitting the mash-out (boost to 168 degrees F following saccharification). This saves about fifteen minutes. On the other hand, the low mash temperature means a very viscous wort, and runoff and recirculation time may be doubled. For this reason I always do a mash-out, even when making British ales by a single-temperature infusion.

I have found that with either lauter tun, the procedure that takes the least time and produces the least amount of frustration is the one that goes against all the conventional wisdom. The best method is, first, to get the runoff going as soon as possible after mashing out, so that the wort does not cool. This is especially important if your lauter tun is not insulated. Second, open the tap full blast and let the wort run off at its own speed. This gives somewhat more packing, but the total time for collecting your wort will be less, because the runoff is so much quicker. A thick mash helps here because less wort needs to be run off before the filter is established, and the bed will be looser.

By the way, I have found that the tap will occasionally get plugged even when it is wide open. If this happens, you should first try closing it for a moment, then reopening it to allow back pressure to flush out the blockage. If that doesn't work, disassembling the spigot is a sure cure and takes only a minute with the plastic "Drum Tap."

I find that I have to collect one to one and a half gallons of sweet wort before the runoff is perfectly clear. By the time this happens, the filter bed is pretty well established. Because the wort is so dense, the runoff is slow at this stage. It helps to heat the cloudy wort to about 160 degrees F before returning it to the lauter tun, but it is even more important to maintain the level of liquid at or above the surface of the grains throughout the operation.

Another thing I have found is that there is no need to be overly cautious about sparging. Once the last of the cloudy wort has been recirculated, you can add up to two quarts of sparge water at a time, deliberately raising the water level well above the surface of the filter bed. This agitates the upper layers, but the wort continues to run clear; and the increased pressure speeds up the flow considerably.

One difference I have noted between the two-bucket lauter tun and the grain bag system is that with the former, the grain mass tends to separate from the side of the bucket as it settles. This means you have to do some "landscaping" during the runoff. Otherwise, a lot of your sparge water will run down this space between the grain bed and the wall of the bucket and will not do its job. This seems to be less of a problem with a canvas grain bag.

Another observation I have made is that any type of lauter tun requires a settling space below the bottom of the tap. This need only be one or two pints, but it is important. Without an adequate settling space, grits will continue to be washed out into the clear wort throughout the sparge. The space should not be too big, since it represents a loss of extract, but it must be there. I have experimented with tilting the tun severely to eliminate it, and the results were unsatisfactory.

I have already indicated my preference for the grain bag over the conventional two-bucket lauter tun. However, I must admit it is a little more expensive and difficult to construct. I feel it is worth the effort, and ready-made bags are now available. However, you can make a plastic-bucket design that works nearly as well. First, select an inner (strainer) bucket that is slightly smaller than the outside one. For my own experiments, I used four-gallon food-grade pails for the strainer buckets and a five-gallon for the outer one. With this arrangement, the inner bucket sits right on the tap and the space between the false and true bottoms is less than two inches. This is important because you don't want the level of wort to sink below the surface of the grains while the mash is sitting in the lauter tun prior to runoff.

The other ploy is to drill the false bottom with slightly larger holes—three-sixteenths rather than one-eighth of an inch. I have made such a strainer recently, and it gives runoff/recirculation times on a par with my grain bag. Its only drawbacks are first, the problem of the filter bed separating from the bucket wall; and second, a tendency for draff to wash through even after the filter is established. A settling space of two pints minimizes this problem.

I think you can see from this presentation that in many respects I have thrown away the book as far as my techniques are concerned. This was never a matter of deliberate intent; it was just the way things worked out as I tried to improve my system. I was looking for speed, but not at the price of efficiency. Also, I wanted to make the mash process as simple as possible. And finally, I wanted to cut frustration and work to a minimum. I believe I have succeeded in meeting these goals.

Table 2 shows a typical schedule for a brewing session in my home. I feel it illustrates two key points about grain brewing. The first is that, even though it takes eight to nine hours, the work required is far less than that figure would suggest. On brewing days I spend most of my time doing other things—reading the paper, playing with my kids, even taking a nap if I feel like it. The second point is that, despite the difficulties I have discussed today, mashing and sparging are simple, routine procedures. Extract brewers who watch me make a batch of wort almost always say something like, "Gee, anybody could do this." Exactly.

The main factor that will continue to limit the popularity of grain brewing is simply the amount of time required. It might be possible, with better malt mills and more expensive equipment to use mashing and sparging

Table 2
Typical Brewing Session

Step	Time	Work time	Explanation
1. Measure & crush malt	30 min.	30 min.	
2. Mash-in & pH adjustment	15 min.	15 min.	
3. Protein rest	30 min.	—	
4. Boost to starch conv.	10 min.	10 min.	
5. Starch conversion	90 min.	10 min.	prepare sparge water
6. Boost to mash-out	10 min.	10 min.	
7. Mash-out	5 min.	5 min.	set-up lauter tun
8. Rest in lauter tun	5 min.	5 min.	set-up for wort collection
9. Runoff & recirculation	40 min.	20 min.	intermittent
10. Sparge	35 min.	10 min.	intermittent

11. Heat wort to boil	30 min.	30 min.	clean-up
12. Boil	90 min.	10 min.	weigh & add hops
13. Settle & strain off	15 min.	10 min.	
14. Chill wort & pitch (immersion cooler)	60 min.	10 min.	intermittent stirring
15. Clean boiler & cooler	10 min.	10 min.	
Totals	8 hrs.	3 hrs. 10 min.	

procedures that would take an hour or two off the schedule, but extract brewing will always be faster.

On the other hand, grain beers are much less expensive for comparable recipes, and grain brewing requires only a modest expenditure for additional equipment. It also offers unlimited opportunities to use a tremendous variety of malts and adjuncts so that you can custom tailor your beers to your own taste. I believe that many more people would be willing to try it if they knew how easy it can be.

Dave Miller

Table 3
Recommendations

For Minimum Extraction:
—Stiff mash
—Lengthy starch conversion (1-2 hours)
—Leave space beneath false bottom empty (do not under let)
—Avoid cracking or separation of filter bed
—Recirculate all cloudy wort before adding sparge water
—Generous sparge (equal to final volume of batch)

For Trouble-free Sparging:
—False bottom or strainer with large-diameter holes (1/4 or 3/16 in.)
—Space below false bottom no more than 2 inches.
—Settling space below tap (1-2 pts.)
—Stiff mash
—Mash-out at 168 degrees F
—Short rest in lauter tun (5 min.)
—Rapid runoff (open tap wide and let wort drain at its own speed)
—Begin recirculation as soon as wort level drops below surface of grains
—Heat cloudy wort to 160 degrees F before recirculating if possible
—Acidify sparge water to pH 5.7
—Hold sparge water at 168 degrees F or lower

Q: How do you measure the pH of your water?
A: I don't have a pH meter, although I am going to hock my

soul to get one if I have to to get one   before the next
brewing season. I have found that the plastic test strips
made by Merck are more reliable and easier to read than
most pH papers.

Q: How much lactic acid do you use, and why do you
recommend it?
A: Lactic acid is a natural product of fermentation and its
molecular structure is very similar to ethyl alcohol. It has
a very mild flavor that is totally compatible with beer. We
are talking about a very small quantity. I can't even use an
eyedropper to adjust the pH of my sparge water with 88
percent lactic acid. Instead I dilute it by mixing 10 cc into
about 750 cc (a standard wine bottle) of tap water. It takes
90 to 115 cc of this dilute acid to drop the pH of my sparge
water to 5.7.

Q: It is a liquid, then.
A: Yes, it is always sold as a liquid. One of the reasons
many suppliers don't want to handle lactic acid is that it
isn't stable in crystalline form. It has to be diluted with at
least a little bit of water, and so it is usually sold commercially at either 88 or 80 percent concentration.

Q: Where can you get lactic acid?
A: I used to get 88 percent lactic from a mail-order house,
but they quit carrying it. I am now getting a product from
England, by way of Wineking, a wholesaler in Oregon. The
bottle doesn't state the dilution, but it is lower than 88
percent, so you might want to use 15 to 20 cc to make up
your bottle of working stock.Most homebrew supply stores
should be able to order it for you.

By the way, while we are on this point, I want to make it clear that I am not advocating the use of lactic acid to decarbonate your water. First you should get rid of as much of the carbonate as you can by other means, then you use the lactic acid to drop the sparge water down to 5.7.

My water supply is treated with lime to remove as much calcium and magnesium as possible. It is a very successful treatment—even a galvanized pipe in our home will last thirty to thirty-five years. It also gets rid of most of the alkalinity so I don't have to boil my water before I brew with it. There is not much wrong with the water, but the pH runs between 9 and 10. If you start sparging with it, the runoff will start at 5.3 or whatever the pH of the mash was. But as the sparge goes on, the pH of the runoff will rise very quickly and you will have the problems I talked about. So even though you don't need to treat the mash water very much--only a little bit of gypsum to drop the pH of a pale malt mash--it is really important to acidify the sparge water.

Almost anybody who lives in a city in the greater Mississippi valley, including the Ohio and the Missouri rivers, has the same basic type of water that I have. Also, most big municipalities in that part of the country treat their water with lime in the way I have described. I know that Kansas City and Cincinnati do, for example.

Q: Do you back-sparge at all, and go through a couple of times?
A: No. Once that runoff clears, I just start collecting the heavy sweet wort in the boiler, and as soon as I have recirculated all the cloudy runoff, I start pouring in the sparge water.

Q: Is there a certain depth or volume of grain that you shoot for?

A: The trouble is, it is not really practical to manipulate that parameter. I mean, most of us are going to use one lauter tun for all of our mashes.

If you are doing five-gallon batches, lauter tuns of nine to ten inches diameter seem to work pretty well with the crush of malt that we get with our Corona mills. If you are talking ten-gallon batches, it is worth your while to seek out bigger buckets with larger surface areas.

I use anywhere between five and twelve pounds of grain for each batch of beer. So obviously the depth of the filter bed varies. If it is very shallow, I am not quite as sloppy about pouring the hot sparge water on as I am when the bed is deeper. You have to exercise a bit of judgment about this. My main point is that you can usually pour the sparge water on and raise the level quite high without breaking up the whole filter bed and prolonging your sparge operation.

Q: Most of the people in our club use a giant-size Coleman ice chest, and then they fit copper in the bottom and slot the copper.

A: That is something I can't address because I never built one of those things. I know they are easy to build; they are also more expensive. One of my interests is trying to make mashing not only as simple as possible but also as inexpensive as possible. I would like to see more homebrewers try it, and I feel a lot of them are held back by what they think is the exorbitant cost of equipment.

I would like to know how big a Coleman do you use,

Dave Miller

and how careful do you have to be about adding the sparge water? Obviously the grain depth is going to be less.

Q: I just bought a square trash can. I took some copper tubing and slotted it and poked it right through the side. The whole thing cost me about $10. But most people in our club use the Coleman 40 or 48 quart models--the big ones. They work for almost any size mash.

A: As I said, obviously you are going to get much less depth to your grain bed with that big surface area, so I thought that probably wouldn't be a good choice for me. I am too impatient to carefully sprinkle the sparge water on the top, trying not to disturb the grain bed at all. It just doesn't fit my personality.

Q: Some people take an aluminum can and poke some holes in the sides. They put that on top of the grain bed and pour the water in. It drains out and does the sprinkling automatically.

A: That's a clever way around it. That would work fine. What I said at the beginning applies here. If you have another setup and it works for you, that's fine.

Taling about the depth of the filter bed reminds me that there is another critical factor here--the percentage of area that actually drains. At commercial breweries the percentage of the area that is actually open on a false bottom is relatively small, about 6 or 7 percent. However, their beds are a lot deeper. My lauter tun has an open area of 12.5 percent. I don't know what you would get with a Coleman chest arrangement.

But what you need to be sure of is that the depth

of your grain bed, and your drainage area, are such that you get a quick enough runoff to establish a good filter bed, one that gives a clean runoff and reasonable sparge times. That's what is really important. is quick enough that the filter bed establishes itself to give a clear runoff, and times that are reasonable. These are the kinds of things that you worry about.

Q: Would you recommend treating the mash water to get the correct pH?
A: The pH of the water is not important. The critical factor is the total alkalinity, the combined amount of carbonate and bicarbonate ions in the water. If that is high, you just have to decarbonate the water. Even for dark beers, I think it is easier and more reliable to decarbonate. If you have water that has, say, 75, 100, 150 ppm of bicarbonate, it is easier to decarbonate the whole load of water that you are going to brew with, and then just add a little calcium carbonate back to your mash. You have to approach this empirically--just a half teaspoon at a time, until the mash pH comes up to where you want it. The reason I think you should do this, even when you are making a dark beer, is because you still want your sparge water to be low in alkalinity and low in pH to avoid leaching tannin and other substances.

Q: You think that the crush of the malt causes trouble. What about preground malt?
A: I have never used it, so I will defer to someone with much more experience here, my friend George Fix. Apparently ,the trouble is that precrushed malt is too vulnerable to bad storage conditions. It tends to soak up atmospheric

Dave Miller

moisture much more readily than the whole malt. So it is best to buy it in small quantities and use it within a week after it arrives if you want to be safe. Of course, if you live in Arizona and the relative humidity is 10 percent, you don't have that problem. I come from St. Louis, where the humidity is over 50 percent all year round, and much higher in certain seasons.

Q: In sparging, do you maintain a level of liquid on the mash, or do you drain it dry and then refill?
A: At the beginning, I just crank the tap wide open and watch the grain mass sink somewhat. Then the level of the grain won't sink any more. You will see that the actual level of sweet wort is starting to go below the surface. My strong feeling is that as soon as this happens, you must begin to recirculate. You don't want the bed to drain dry. You recirculate all the cloudy wort before you start adding sparge water. But throughout the entire operation, you keep the liquid level at or above the surface of the bed.

Q: To increase the porosity of the filter, especially when you are using adjuncts such as wheat that have a high protein content and make the wort very viscous, I was considering saving some of the spent grains from my last batch, boiling the daylights out of them-- possibly in a very alkaline solution to remove as many of the tannins as possible, rinsing and drying them, and then saving them for reuse to add porosity to the filter bed.
A: All I can say is, please write and tell me what your results are! That is not a negative comment. I just mean that, for better or worse, I don't have enough dedication to do that. It sounds in theory like a very sound, ingenious

method, and I would not be surprised if some commercial breweries do something like that. I have in the past had a devil of a time with my sparging when I am making any kind of beer with flaked barley as an adjunct. Apparently it is not only protein content, but the beta-glucan fraction that causes the trouble. Especially with unmalted barley, it is very high, and that stuff is really gummy. That is one reason I use a longer protein rest with those kinds of grist.It is not only for the protein; it is to give the beta-glucanase in the malt every opportunity to break down the beta glucan so you don't have a problem with the runoff. .

Q: Do you try to keep the acidity constant in your recipes? Would you recommend adding acid to the mash to keep the total acid the same?
A: I don't think that is important. My approach is totally empirical. I mash in in straight tap water, wait a couple of minutes, then measure the pH of the mash. If it is too high, I chuck in a quarter or maybe half a teaspoon of gypsum, and that always brings it down; I never need to use more than that. If it is too low, I add calcium carbonate to try to bring it up.

I have found that the mash will work pretty well between 5.0 and 5.5, so I will accept anything in there. I can usually manage that. I always treat the sparge water exactly the same. I acidify it with a very small quantity of lactic acid-- so small that you can't taste the lactic acid in the sparge water. It may have a little bit different feel on the tongue than it did before because alkalinity gives a kind of slick feel to the water. Lactic acid makes it feel a little cleaner and squeakier, but other than that, it is completely tasteless. For this reason, I don't think the exact amount matters.

If you are dealing with a water supply that has not been decarbonated by the water company, you are in a different position. You should decarbonate that water before you use it. Preferably you should boil and rack it. Otherwise, you will have to use a lot of acid, and that might affect the flavor.

Q: I use filtered water.
A: Well, it depends on what kind of filtration. The water companies all filter the water also. You can use filters to get rid of excess chlorine, for instance, but the alkalinity of the water still has to be right. Most of the breweries want a slightly alkaline water because an acid water is a disaster. It can dissolve zinc out of the coating of galvanized pipes. My water company is perfectly happy to have pH of 9 or 10 for the water. And since the water is low in bicarbonate, the local brewery is happy, too.

Q: You mentioned saving time during the sparge. Have you ever considered omitting the protein rest of the mash?
A: Apparently that is the trend of the future, even in lager brewing. The schedule I gave was for lager because that's mostly what I brew, and I am still chicken-hearted enough to want to do a half-hour protein rest when I am working with lager malt. But more and more breweries, including German breweries, are mashing in at higher temperatures, and are essentially going with a single-temperature mash. Apparently there isn't much protein breakdown that goes on during that so-called protein rest. What actually happens is protein precipitation, which can take place any time, even at a higher temperature. This applies

to an all-mal, a malt-and-rice, or a malt-and-corn type of grist. I am a lot more reluctant to give up that low tempera-ture rest if I am also incorporating wheat malt or flaked barley in my grist because of the beta glucans and glycoproteins those materials contain.

Q: When you make a wheat beer, how do you go about getting a starch conversion?

A: This is something that has been argued back and forth in the pages of zymurgy. The standard advice, which I also give in my own book, is don't count on the wheat malt. Use at least a third lager malt, prefreably six-row,to be sure that you have enough alpha and beta amylase to do your starch conversion. I use a low-temperature starch rest (150F) and a two-hour rest to get total conversion. I also grind the wheat malt pretty fine

Apparently a lot depends on the wheat malt. Dif-ferent types vary enormously in their enzyme potential depending not only on how they were kilned, but also on the variety. The stuff that I get from my local supplier is British wheat malt, and based on my experience with British pale malt. Based on what I know about British kilning schedules, and the low enzyme content of pale ale malt, I don't trust it. I always use at least a third lager malt in the mash.

Q: Are you talking about malt?

A: Wheat malt, yes. I am not talking about wheat flakes. Obviously, with flaked wheat, you have to be even more careful about getting enough enzymes into your mash. I would not recommend using two-thirds wheat flakes; I probably wouldn't go over 40 percent. By the way, that also goes for brewing flour, which is a coarse-ground whole wheat flour that a lot of British breweries use with a great deal of assuranc

Q: Some of the wheat that you can buy at health food stores has an enormously high protein content, and we have had experience with incredibly gummy mashes. Also, the gluten used to make bread is bad for beer.
A: Yes. High-gluten flour is probably the very worst kind of thing that you could use. I would probably stick to malted wheat, or the wheat flakes or brewing flour supplied to the commercial brewers.

Dave Miller earned the 1981 American Homebrewers Association Homebrewer of the Year Award. He has more than eleven years' experience in homebrewing and is the author of The Complete Handbook of Home Brewing.

One of 100s of volunteers
at the Great American
Beer Festival.

4.
Aroma Identification

Charlie Papazian
American Homebrewers Association
Gregory Noonan
Author of Brewing Lager Beer

Gregory Noonan was originally going to give this talk, but unfortunately, or fortunately, the state of Vermont passed a law allowing brewpubs and Greg is there working on his brewpub right now. Greg did a lot of the groundwork for this presentation, which is a different format from anything we have presented at a conference like this. I will be giving the presentation and then participants will go to stations around the room—sniff stations, you might call them—where they can compare the odors of doctored beer along with some standard samples we have here. This will give participants an opportunity to experience first hand some things they have heard or read about. But first, I will read Greg Noonan's short introduction about what aroma is.

"Before we taste beer, our olfactory receptors perceive the aroma of beer. That aroma plays a very important part in how we evaluate beer's flavor. The workshop

here will present standards for aroma identification based on the reference standards specified by Dr. Morton Meilgaard of the Stroh Brewing Company. Dr. Meilgaard has done years and years of research on flavor and aroma evaluation. He led the joint American Society of Brewing Chemists and the European Brewing Congress Subcommittee on Sensory Analysis in the identification of major sensory stimulants in beer, and he developed a Beer Flavor Terminology System supported by appropriate reference standards.

"Only by training our olfactory sense and taste buds to recognize particular smells and tastes and to identify these by specific terms can we as judges, beer evaluators, brewers, and beer drinkers ever hope to communicate to one another something specific about our likes and dislikes of a given brew.

"When you begin to understand what Dr. Meilgaard and his associates have made possible, you can really appreciate how valuable this information is. For example, in one study that is indicative of the training it takes to understand what flavor and aroma are about, in a group of university students, 14 percent mistakenly identified citric acid as "bitter" and 8 percent called quinine sulfate in solution "sour," although it is very bitter. That is like telling somebody whose house is painted red, that it is yellow. We communicate better with our sense of sight, but our senses of smell and taste are often taken for granted.

"As beer evaluators, particularly if you are involved with judging beer, you understand that you taste certain things in beer. Yet, how do you communicate that flavor? If someone says a beer tastes of dimethyl sulfide

(DMS) does he mean to say it has a skunky flavor? Or is he really talking about a sulfury or winey character? Knowing how to make those identifications of flavor or aroma takes practice. This is what this presentation is about.

"The Beer Flavor Terminology System enables us to relate beer identification terms to sensations, giving us a common language framework within which to communicate about beer and point out ways for us to improve our beer. The work that has produced this system, is no small accomplishment. Isolating major stimulants—in all, 120 of them in fourteen classes—involves resolving regional and even international semantic disparities, investigating, identifying, testing, and accepting or rejecting possible standards. It includes establishing threshold sensitivity and appropriate standard concentration for these compounds.

"As an indication of its importance, I would like to point out that the American Society of Enology and Viticulture has adopted Dr. Meilgaard's work in a Wine Aroma Wheel and standardized Wine Aroma Terminology and Standards. Malting and Brewing Science, a technical book on brewing, devotes pages to it, and it is often referred to in other publications, magazines, and journals. It is as useful a tool as any piece of brewing equipment.

"Why is this so? Because for the most part, smell is an untrained sense. The ability to smell odors is incredibly acute. Humans can smell minute concentrations of aromatic compounds, often in as little as parts per billion. If we are trained to recognize specific aromas, and to relate those to brewing processes or ingredients, we can correct deficiencies in our beer's flavor and aroma. As judges we can go beyond our likes and dislikes and recognize

Flavor Wheel showing class terms and first-tier terms.

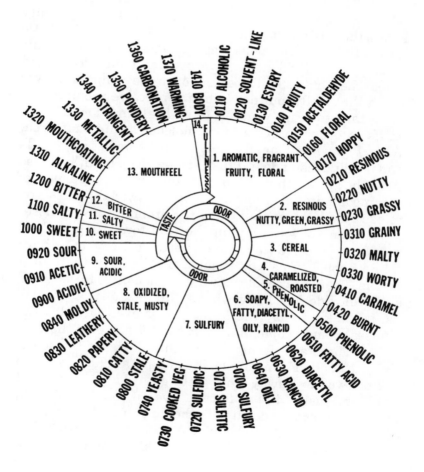

whether an entry is appropriate or inappropriate within a stylistic category."

-Greg Noonan

There is, however, a correct method for sniffing beer to gain maximum olfactory sensation. In our olfactory sense, there is an olfactory cleft. What I liken it to is a little pocket that receives molecules of aroma and sends signals to the brain. Evidently, from articles I have read and researched, only about 4 percent of aroma compounds ever reach that cleft. In order to better perceive aromas, it is important to train yourself to sniff at an odor in short sniffs in order to bring more molecules into that area. What I do when I smell a beer is take short strong sniffs and if that doesn't do it, I take strong, deep breaths. I also swirl the glass—that is again another important aspect of gaining maximum aroma for when you swirl the glass, you release the bubbles that carry the aroma into your nose.

Some of you sampling these doctored beers will not be able to perceive what others perceive. Some of us have "blind spots" to certain smells, particularly the sulfur smells. There are people who are not sensitive to, let's say, sulfur dioxide. You know what sulfur dioxide is; to most of us, it stinks, to say the least, and it even irritates the sinuses. Some people, however, cannot perceive that.

There are circumstances that decrease the sensitivity to odors. For example, if you have a cold, or you are one or two days away from getting a cold, your sense of smell and taste will be affected. Even if you don't feel ill, but you are coming down with the flu or a cold, your sense of flavor and smell can be affected one or two days before you come down with it. Likewise, certain vitamin deficien-

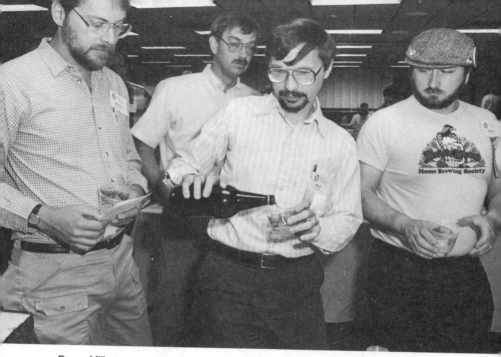

Dave Miller pours samples of beer doctored with various flavor and aroma compounds. They allow brewers to learn to identify which odors they are sensitive or "blind" to.

cies can affect your sensitivity to smell and aroma. Eating certain foods will affect your sensitivity to smell and taste. Some research has shown ingesting alcohol or sugar diminishes your ability to smell. On the other hand, acids and things that are sour or bitter—such as red wine and coffee—can enhance your ability to perceive flavors and aromas.

(For additional information on how to produce beer samples, please see Table 8 in Chapter 1, Sensory Evaluation for Brewers.)

I would like to caution you, before I tell you about the doctored beers, that these are not to be tasted. They are to be smelled only. Some of the additives in the beers are poisonous. I experimented last week in my home with doctoring some beers, and I must tell you that if you plan

BEER AROMA RECOG-

by Charlie Papazian

(much of this data is from Dr. Morton Meilgaard's work on the

Mielgaard Ref. No.	General Descriptor	Technical Descriptor
0110	Alcoholic	Alcohol
0111	Clove	Spicy
0112	Winey	Fusely, Vinous
0123	Solvent-like	Acetone
0133	Estery, Fruity, Solvent	Ethyl Acetate
0150	Green Apples	Acetaldehyde
0220	Sherry	Sherry
0224	Almond, Nutty	Nutty
0503	Medicinal, Bandaid-like, Plastic-like	Phenolic
620	Butter, Butterscotch	Diacetyl
0710	Sulfury	Sulfitic, Sulfur dioxide
0721	Skunky, lightstruck	Skunky
0732	Sweet corn, cabbage	Dimethylsulfide/DMS
0800	Stale, Cardboard	Stale, Oxidation
0910	Sour/Vinegar	Acetic (acid)
0920	Sour/Lactic	Lactic (acid)

Note: *some of these substances are poisonous and should **not** be tasted*

NITION GUIDELINES
and Greg Noonan
subject and Charlie Papazian's experience with handling samples)

Substance Used for Recognition Training	Concentration in 12 oz. beer *(prepare samples 12-24 hours before using)*	Concentration one quart beer
Ethanol	15 ml	40 ml
Eugenol	100 micrograms	265 micrograms
Allspice	2 g	5 g
Cloves	(marinate cloves in beer)	
Gallo Chablis	1 fl. oz.	2.7 fl. oz.
Laquer thinner	.03 ml	.08 ml
Ethyl Acetate	.028 ml	.076 ml
Acetaldehyde	.016 ml or 16 mg	.040 ml or 40 mg
Sherry	1.25 fl. oz.	3.25 fl. oz.
Benzaldehyde	.002 ml or 2 mg	.005 ml or 5 mg
Almond Extact	4 drops	11 drops
Phenol	.003 ml or 3 mg	.010 ml or 10 mg
Diacetyl	.00005 ml	.00014 ml
Butter flavor extract	4 drops	11 drops
Sodium or Pottasium Metabisulfite	20 mg	50 mg
Beer exposed to light		
Dimethylsulfide/DMS (Note: unstable)	.00003 ml or 30 micrograms	.0001 ml or 100 micrograms
Heat sample for one week at 90°-100° F. or marinate cardboard in beer		
White Vinegar	7.5 ml	25 ml
Lactic Acid	.4 ml	1.1 ml

to make one of these aroma identification kits, please get written permission from your spouse or roommate first. Some of these odors can lead to dissension. The terrible odors can linger three days or longer. If you are going to put together some samples, find someone who has a laboratory with a good ventilation system. Otherwise you are going to be living with almondy smell, diacetyl or the lacquer thinner smell of ethyl acetate for three days. It isn't pleasant at all.

The other thing that is difficult in putting together these kits is that many of these aromas are very volatile and unstable. It is suggested that these concentrations be put into beer samples only twelve to twenty-four hours before they are actually sampled. Otherwise, many of them are so volatile and unstable that their propensities will diminish. Because of my Conference schedule,I was unable to do that for this session, and made these samples forty-eight to seventy hours ago. I'm curious to see how intense some of these things will turn out.

In preparing these samples, I noticed that if I followed the guidelines for the amount of additive in twelve ounces of beer, some of the samples were too strong, and some were much too weak as far as my senses are concerned. So I want to share with you and make some important changes here as far as my own findings indicated. For example, I boosted the eugenol up to 100 micrograms in a twelve-ounce sample. But I cut the acetone down to .03 milliliters. I had a very difficult time perceiving ethyl acetate and multiplied the original standard by four, to .028. On the acetaldehyde, the green-apples character, I multiplied by eight, to.016 milliliters. I increased the sodium metabisulfite to 20 milligrams.

The Beer Judge Certification Program honored the first five men to achieve the status of National Judge. Shown with their certificates are William Pfeiffer (left), David Norton, Richard Gleeson, and Scott Birdwell. (Ted Whippie was absent.) Presenting the awards are Charlie Papazian (far left), Jim Homer (second from right), and Pat Baker.

One sample I wasn't able to produce was lactic acid. Lactic does not have, I believe, an aroma in and of itself. Other by-products produced by bacteria produce lactic acid in beer. Here I am arguing with Dr. Meilgaard without first asking for an explanation. I shouldn't be doing that; there probably is some character, but I can't perceive it.

You will also see the chart, Beer Aromas and Their Possible Sources. This can be very useful to us as brewers as it tells us how we can improve our beer and how we can improve our comments when we evaluate other peoples' beer. As a professional brewer, you should be able to recognize certain flavors or aromas that you may be blind to. You may be making a beer with a strong diacetyl character to it, and if you are blind to that, you will never

Beer Aromas and Their Possible Sources
by Greg Noonan and Charlie Papazian

0110	Alcoholic	High starting gravity, excessive attenuation
0111	Clove	Characteristic of wheat beer; if excessive, wild-yeast contamination
0112	Winey	From oxidation, except strong lagers or barley wines
0123	Solvent-like	From warm fermentation, plastic, wild yeast, common in old estery ales
0133	Estery, Fruity, Solvent	From warm fermentation, yeast strain, too few yeast nutrients
0150	Green Apples	High fermentation temperature, insufficient yeast pitched, beer racked too early
0220	Sherry	Warm fermentation or oxidation, very old beer
0224	Almond, Nutty	Oxidation, very old beer
0503	Medicinal/Phenolic	From water supply, chlorine residue, plastic, wild yeast, improper sparging techniques
0620	Butter/Diacetyl	High initial fermentation temperature, racked, cooled or fined too soon, pedicoccus contamination
0710	Sulfury, SO_2	Wild yeast contamination
0721	Skunky	Beer exposed to light
0732	Sweet corn, DMS	Insufficient kettle boil, wort chilled too slowly, coliform bacteria contamination
0800	Stale, cardboard	From oxidation of amino acids during aging, at bottling, in bottle, old beer—heat accelerates the process
0910	Sour vinegar	Acetobacter contamination
0920	Sour-lactic	Lactobacillus contamination

detect it. That is why all breweries should have a panel of tasters, not just a brewmaster. There are some very competent brewmasters who are blind to diacetyl. But the wise ones know that they are! It is very important for all brewers, and particularly commercial operations, to have an objective, trained panel to taste and smell the beer. What these doctored samples do is to begin that training.

The equipment I used to make these samples was not very sophisticated. I used a pipette, which is a long graduated cylinder. To make a concentration of one part per million, take a sample of your chemical and dilute it one in one hundred milliliters of distilled water. Then dilute one milliliter of that solution into a hundred milliliters of distilled water—that gives you one part in ten thousand. By continuing this dilution process, you can easily get concentrations measurable in parts per million and parts per billion.

Some of the chemicals used to doctor these samples were obtained from chemical companies Others are obtainable through grocery stores, and household items stores. Some are not very soluble in water. In that case, I use a capful of grain (ethnyol) alcohol in a beaker with the high-concentration solution and dissolve the chemicals in the alcohol before I add the distilled water. Otherwise there are globs of oil floating around.

Some people have suggested that the American Homebrewers Association put together these kits, but after my experience with this, I don't think the AHA wants to be in that business. But if there is anyone who wants to put together kits for twelve-ounce bottles, understanding which chemicals are stable and which are unstable, we would be glad to work something out to make it available through the AHA. It is something a lot of people have asked me for through the years.

One word of caution: we have to be careful not to define all of these taste sensations as bad. I feel that if any of these are too strong, then they are bad. In tiny, minute amounts, however, they may add character to an otherwise bland-tasting beer. So in beers where the flavor level is really low, like most mass-produced beers, most of these characteristics may be perceived as bad. In full brews, however, like the ones you are making, many of these flavor components might very well be desirable.

For example, the clove characteristic—a characteristic of Bavarian wheat beer—is desirable for that style. Diacetyl in American Pilsener style, is not at all appropriate, but in certain styles of ales, particularly English pale ales, a certain amount of that can be very nice. Too much, and you need to figure out ways to cut back on it. That is a call that is up to the brewer. DMS is generally a characteristic of most lagers, and at almost imperceptible levels. It adds the flavor and aroma that makes a lager a lager. Yet having DMS in an ale may not be appropriate.

Let me take a moment to tell you how to go about sampling these doctored beers or conducting a sampling session at your club. The samples around the room have a piece of paper describing each one. There are approximately ten cups beside each bottle, and those cups should not leave the vicinity of that beer. In other words, don't take a sample of diacetyl across the room and sample it. Sample it in that area so we don't get things confused.

In a separate area, there are ten bottles of Coors beer at room temperature. The Coors beer is your standard sample to take around the room with you. This way, when you go to the various sample stations, you can compare what Coors is compared to the doctored sample. I chose Coors because it's local, fresh, and light.

You don't need very much of the doctored samples in a glass. Perhaps only an ounce. You want to leave enough room in the glass so that you can swirl the doctored beer around to get the volatiles out of the glass.

Charlie Papazian is publisher of zymurgy, *president of the Amercian Homebrewers Association, and the designer of dozens of noted beer recipes.*

Gregory Noonan is a long-time homebrewer, the author of Brewing Lager Beer, *and a frequent contributor to both* The New Brewer *and* zymurgy. *He is also the proud developer of a brewpub in Burlington, Vermont.*

George Marti pours his
award-winning August Schell beer.

5.
The Excitement Is Brewing

Hans Bilger
Brewmaster, Oldenberg Brewery

What I have to say is in a lighter vein than many of the talks here. I want to tell you about being a brewmaster in a microbrewery, about the joy of brewing.

Professional brewmasters have a tendency to be a little on the pompous side, but please don't feel that I act in a pompous manner when I tell you that, as a professional brewer, it is really an experience for me to listen in on some of the presentations here at this conference. The level of knowledge here humiliates some professional brewers. I think quite a few of you homebrewers would stand up very well in the environment of professional brewing. I think it is wonderful that hands-on tradesmanship in brewing is coming back.

I get a big thrill out of this because I am an old tradesman. My family had a brewery in southern Germany that was founded in 1821. We always have felt that tradesmanship as a brewer is something to be proud of. I

went to Weihenstephan and have a degree in brewery engineering. That is something like a masters degree in chemical engineering, but rather than cracking hydrocarbons, we brewed beer and designed breweries.

In order to call myself a braumeister, however, I had to serve an apprenticeship for three years, which means that I spent three years with brush in hand scouring the brown scale that forms in wooden kegs. I wielded the brush this way and that in a very hands-on type of training. Sometimes even now I wake up in the middle of the night still thinking, "Oof! I have to take that professional exam for the master brewery again!" I don't mean the university exam, but the brush-in-hand exam where young brewers had to clean the barrel under the eagle eyes of some old brewmaster. Those old brewmasters relished making things hard for us.

I wake up sweating and protesting, "But I already passed!"

We in the brewing industry today are pioneers of a new trend, the trend of hand-crafted beer. I don't want to be in any way derogatory to mass production because thanks to mass production we have achieved a very sophisticated living standard. We are living better than all humans before us in terms of material wealth. There is something amiss, however, and until recently, very few people could specify what it is that we are missing. We can afford almost anything we want, so what is amiss? I think we miss a certain romance in our lives. People need romance; it is what makes us human. And this romance is something that mass production can't deliver.

When I started at Oldenberg Brewery, it was like lightning had struck me when I noticed how visitors to the

Bilger-Bräu seit 1821
In vierter Bilger-Folge

Hans Bilger's family has been in brewing since 1821. Shown is the Bilger Brewery in Germany, built in 1912. Hans is the brewmaster at Oldenberg Brewery in Ft. Mitchell, Kentucky.

brewery loved the setting. When they visited with me, their eyes radiated. They loved the beer; they loved everything about it. There is a certain quality of life that all of us in this small setting have that huge breweries can never have. I am very happy to be involved with this because it enhances the quality of all of our lives.

How I came to be involved in brewing is through my family. We had a little brewery in the beautiful town of Gottmadingen, Germany, near Lake Constance.

In 1912, the family built a new brewhouse and nearly went bankrupt because it was so huge. Fortunately, the inflation after World War I helped a lot, and its glory peaked just before the Second World War.

Can you imagine the work that went into shoveling tons of malt and scrubbing the storage tanks? The fermenters were open because at that time, it was deemed undesirable to have closed fermenters. It seemed very important that the foam and brown hop resins rose to the surface during fermentation so they could be removed. Today, thinking there has changed, but I am sure there are still some brewers who would not do without open fermenters.

Hans as a young, apprentice brewer.

The brewery was my life when I was growing up. I could see it from my window when I woke up in the morning and when I went to bed at night. Then I went to university to learn more about brewing. During my days at Weihenstephan, I used to crawl through a little hole in the kegs and scrape off the sludge.

After working in many breweries in Germany, I came to the United States to learn the wonderful ways of American breweries and mass-produced beer. I worked for Pabst for many years, and then when Pabst started closing one brewery after another, I went out of the brewing business for a few years. I really missed it, but in the late Seventies, breweries were closing everywhere and I thought to myself, "Unfortunately the romance of life is gone, and maybe you should look elsewhere."

I was into soda pop manufacturing when I heard that a microbrewery was being started in Kentucky and its owners were looking for a brewmaster. Then I believed

The Oldenberg Brewery, located in Ft. Mitchell, Kentucky, is a modern hotel/restaurant/brewery complex with Old World grace and style. It is the site of the 1989 Conference on Quality Beer and Brewing.

that my luck was picking up. The building at Oldenberg is very complex and would never have been built by a very large corporation because of concern for the immediate return on investments. Something like Oldenberg doesn't immediately offer huge returns to its stockholders. And yet I believe that small corporations are beginning to put money into small but excellent facilities like Oldenberg.

Oldenberg is a hotel/restaurant/brewery complex. A few years ago, the investors wanted to build a convention complex, but new convention centers were being built right and left. Oldenberg's owners wanted something special to enhance the complex—something that would set it apart from the others. They considered a dinner theater, but David Heidrich, the youngest member of the family, wanted to build a brewery. Everybody laughed at first, but a few weeks later the idea was taken up in earnest, and the brewery was built. One of the most important missions of that brewery is to provide enhancement to the people business. It provides a tourist attraction, if you want to call it that. We try to make a contribution to the quality of life of the people who come to visit.

The brewery was built by Enerfab, which is one of the most influential builders of brewery equipment in the United States. Enerfab has done a lot of work for megabreweries, and ours was the first small brewery Enerfab built. They used the standards of sophistication being used in very large breweries. Our lauter tun is just like the lauter tun at Anheuser Busch, just scaled down a bit. It is just great to work with good equipment. I am sure you homebrewers could work wonders with equipment like this. Everything in the brewhouse is highly computerized, and we can control the entire brewing process from a console.

Every brew is about twenty-five barrels. We have twenty unitanks (combined fermenter-storage tanks) with conical bottoms for two brews each, and two bright beer tanks for our filtered beer.

We filter our beer with a Velo diatomaceous earth filter, which works very well. One very interesting instrument we have is a Witteman pinpoint carbonator. It is a very popular instrument at large breweries, where it is two or three inches in diameter and pumps enormous amounts of beer. We wanted a Witteman carbonator for Oldenberg, but Witteman didn't make them small enough to suit our purpose. For awhile, we lived with carbonating stones in the tank, but we kept calling Witteman and begging them to help us. We were one of those squeaky wheels that draw attention, and when they learned that there might be a market for a smaller unit, they allowed us to pioneer one of their instruments. It works great. Now there are one-inch pinpoint carbonators that are very efficient in microbreweries because you simply dial the carbonation level you desire and you get it.

The pin-point carbonator works by carbonating the beer as it flows through. There are two nozzles, one in the back of the pipe and one in the front, and each inject a very thin, very concentrated point of carbonation into the beer. The stream isn't pointed like a needle, but it is a very concentrated source of high-pressure bubbles. The carbonation is very well dissolved in the beer. It is a really good system.

The temperature of the beer is very important, as is the amount of pressure. The warmer the beer, the higher the pressure must be in order to get good carbonation. The optimum temperature is as cold as you can get it. We work with about 33 degrees F. From solubility tables, we determine the pressure, although we have found that we need a little more pressure than the solubility tables call for because you have to overcome resistance. But once you have empirically determined the amount of pressure you need, you easily can repeat it. You just dial it in, and you know exactly what comes up. The beer passes through the carbonation on the way from filtration at the rate of something like twenty to thirty gallons per minute, and comes out predictably carbonated.

We have a small laboratory where we do a little research and quite a lot of quality control testing.

We have a Simonazzi sixteen-valve filler. I believe that ours is the smallest bottler that Simonazzi makes and

Hans Bilger pours a sample of his Oldenberg Premium Verum, which took Fourth Place in the Consumer Preference Poll at the Great American Beer Festival.

their others are capable of filling something like 2,000 bottles per minute. Sometimes I get calls from people wanting to borrow a spare part for their bottler. They are running 1,800 per minute and we are running 80.

As the bottle goes into the filler, it is subjected to a very high vacuum, something like 90 percent vacuum, and then carbon dioxide is injected into the bottle. This gives a very high percentage of carbon dioxide in the bottle before the beer goes in.

Normally we have six people in the brewery, myself included, but on bottling days, which are once or twice a week, we pull in some additional people from the hotel staff.

We have a semi-automatic keg washing system. The kegs are first blown out with air and then washed with hot caustic solution and steamed, then filled by hand.

We have a replica of a 1921 beer truck that we use for promotionals. We can tap twenty-seven kegs at one time from it. As you can guess, this truck is very popular.

The Oldenberg Complex has been quality built and furnished throughout. The owners bought the world's largest collection of breweriana that was looked at by the Smithsonian and some institutions of similar prestige. But in the final decision, the collection's owners decided to sell it to Oldenberg because there it would be shown. There is even an old grant from a brewhouse and an old keg rack.

We have a wonderful Great Hall that seats 600 diners. The high ceiling and glass give a feeling of spaciousness and gracefulness reminiscent of royalty dinners.

There is one funny story I want to tell you about our weathervane. The weathervane is off the top of the Wiederman brewery, which was in Newport and was the last Kentucky brewery. About three years ago we were building Oldenberg at the same time Heileman was tearing down the brewery and we wanted the old weathervane for Oldenberg. It is something like twelve feet tall and eight feet across and has a beer barrel on top. Oldenberg offered $5,000 for the weathervane. but there was some sentimentality and advertising potential in it and Heileman brought in a crane and took it off the eight-story building and sent it to La Crosse. About a year ago there was a garage sale at La Crosse, and Heileman emptied out all their warehouses of things they hadn't used. We went to La Crosse and bought the weathervane at an auction for $50. Now it sits atop Oldenberg.

What we have tried to do with the entire Oldenberg

Complex and with our beers is to go for quality. For example, our beer is made to emulate beers you would find in a small-town in Bavaria. It is not hugely hopped because Bavarian-type beer is not huge on hops. It is nice and malty. I get a lot of compliments on it from the people who come to visit. I am not boasting, I just want you to know what makes life good for a brewer—that makes for the joy in brewing and for quality life.

Hans Bilger is Master Brewer of the Oldenberg Brewery in Ft. Mitchell, Kentucky. Born in West Germany, Hans studied brewing at "the Harvard of brewing schools," the Technical University Munich at Weihenstephan. He is a fifth generation brewmaster.

Mellie Pullman, Brewmaster
at Schirf Brewing Co.

6.
Improved Record-Keeping

Randy Mosher
Homebrewer

I want to speak to you about keeping records on your homebrewing activities and the benefits of being organized in your brewing efforts. Those people who know me find a certain irony in this since I have never been known as a well-organized person. People never say, "Why can't I be organized like he is?"

This was true until I found homebrewing.

When Ray Spangler and I began homebrewing four years ago, we started with extracts, as most people do. The first batches were, like most people's, not too great. By the time we figured out some of the many things we were doing wrong, we realized that homebrewing was going to be a very complicated hobby. It seemed to me that even writing out the recipe each time was going to be either very tedious, or very simple but incomplete.

Being a graphic designer by training, I started working on a simple recipe sheet that would accommodate

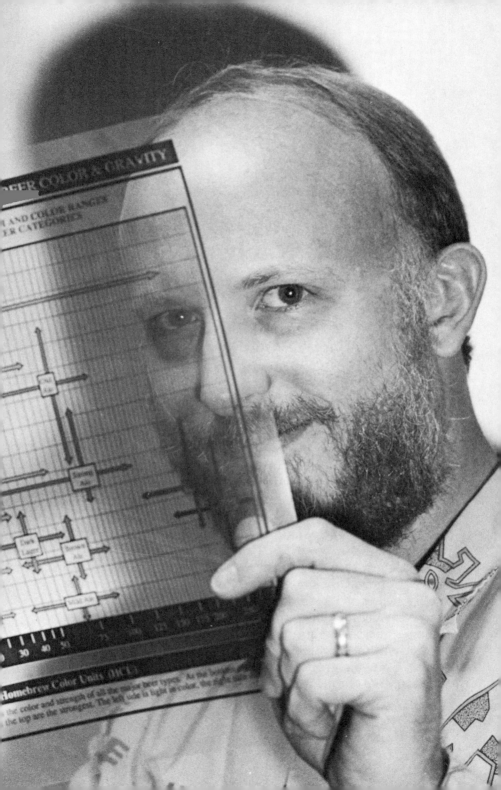

the notes we wanted to make on any given batch of beer. In devising the sheet, it seemed logical to me to follow the time sequence of the brewing process, starting by listing the ingredients and ending with the finished, conditioned beer. You can see from these early examples our first versions. But as our level of brewing expertise increased, the sheets grew with us. Finally, the project got totally out of hand, and now it forms the nucleus of *The Brewer's Workbook* which is in the process of being published.

Worksheets

A comprehensive record-keeping system will allow you to brew exactly the kind of beer you want, and probably help you brew it better as well. Keeping track of the many variables can be a big aid to understanding them, especially how each affects the finished beer.

I believe that the all-important measurements that form the basis of any given beer are color, original gravity, and bitterness. When formulating recipes, they are the targets you should try to hit first. Most of the characteristics that determine a beer's style come from these three measurements. Fermentation type also is critical to beer flavor but does not necessarily require a lot of recipe planning and calculating.

Color vs. Gravity

Let's consider the beer universe with regard to color. The chart here plots beer color along the horizontal axis, and original gravity along the verticle. Lighter ales and lagers are at the lower left, dark; moderate-gravity porters and stouts are at the lower right; and the stronger beers are at the top, left or right, according to color.

BEER TYPE: **Brown Bitter Ale**

RECIPE FROM:_____ P._

STARTED: 4/15/84 RACKED TO SECONDARY 4/27/

BOTTLED: 5/8/84 READY TO DRINK / /

I N G R E D I E N T S

EXTRACT: Qty. **3.3#** Brand **John Bull Amber**

GRAINS: Light_____ Med **1# Crystal**

Dark_____ Adjunct_____

Sugar: Qty. **1 1/2** Type **Dextrose / Brn. Sugar**

HOPS: Bitter **Bullion (1oz)** Finish **Fuggles (2oz)**

YEAST **Old Danish Ale** Finings **I.M.**

OTHER: Priming Sugar 2ᶜ

SPECIFIC GRAVITY CHART

DAY#	1	2	3	4	5	6	7	8	9	10	11	12	13	14	15	16
1.120																
1.110																
1.100																
1.090																
1.080																
1.070																
1.060																
1.050																
1.040	•															
1.030																
1.020																
1.010			•		•											
1.000																
0.990																

(DAY/TIME)

TEMP: Primary 60-64°F Secondary 56° Bottle_____

YIELD: 2c+6 12oz_____ 750ML_____ Other

NOTES_____

RECIPE WORKSHEET — 4 ◆ The Brewer's Workbook

NAME					NAME				
BEER TYPE					BEER TYPE				
DESCRIPTION					DESCRIPTION				
BATCH SIZE					BATCH SIZE				

QTY	GRAVITY	INGREDIENT		COLOR	QTY	GRAVITY	INGREDIENT		COLOR
		◄TOTAL	◄÷NO GAL =HCU◄				◄TOTAL	◄÷NO GAL =HCU◄	

QTY	HOP VARIETY	A ACID	TIME	UNITS	QTY	HOP VARIETY	A ACID	TIME	UNITS

◄HOP BITTERING UNITS = Units x 10.75÷ Gals ◄   ◄HOP BITTERING UNITS = Units x 10.75÷ Gals ◄

MASH TYPE	DILUTION	QT/LB	MASH TYPE	DILUTION	QT/LB
WATER	TREATED TO		WATER	TREATED TO	
MASH			MASH		
BOIL	YEAST		BOIL	YEAST	

NAME					NAME				
BEER TYPE					BEER TYPE				
DESCRIPTION					DESCRIPTION				
BATCH SIZE					BATCH SIZE				

QTY	GRAVITY	INGREDIENT		COLOR	QTY	GRAVITY	INGREDIENT		COLOR
		◄TOTAL	◄÷NO GAL =HCU ◄				◄TOTAL	◄÷NO GAL =HCU ◄	

QTY	HOP VARIETY	A ACID	TIME	UNITS	QTY	HOP VARIETY	A ACID	TIME	UNITS

◄HOP BITTERING UNITS = Units x 10.75 ÷ Gals ◄   ◄HOP BITTERING UNITS = Units x 10.75 ÷ Gals ◄

MASH TYPE	DILUTION	QT/LB	MASH TYPE	DILUTION	QT/LB
WATER	TREATED TO		WATER	TREATED TO	
MASH			MASH		

Color is marked-off in what I am calling Homebrew Color Unit. They are simply the sums of the EBC colors of the various malt types times the number of pounds each, divided by the total number of gallons in the recipe. It is very much like calculating Homebrew Bitterness Units (HBU), using hop quantities and alpha acid content. Some of you may be more familiar with Lovibond numbers. When I started putting all this together, the numbers I had access to were the European EBC figures. Just divide EBC numbers for grain color by two to get the Lovibond numbers. It should be noted that EBC and Lovibond beer colors are quite different and do not really correlate.

Hop Rate vs. Gravity

The chart for Hop Rate vs. Gravity plots hop bitterness along the horizontal axis and original gravity along the verticle. The numbers correspond to the beers listed below. The bitterness levels here are International Hop Bittering Units (IHBU), and not HBUs, by the way. What I have tried to show is hop bitterness as it relates to beer strength. The diagonal lines on the chart divide the world of beers into five arbitrary categories. You can see the malty beers towards the left of the chart, including ones like the Munich lagers and brown ales. At the right are the more markedly bitter beers, such as Pilseners and saisons.

When you are formulating a recipe, the bitterness needed to balance the malt varies according to the gravity of the wort. Two beers of different gravities can have drastically different hop-to-malt-balance, even with the same measured amount of bitterness. We all try to prac-

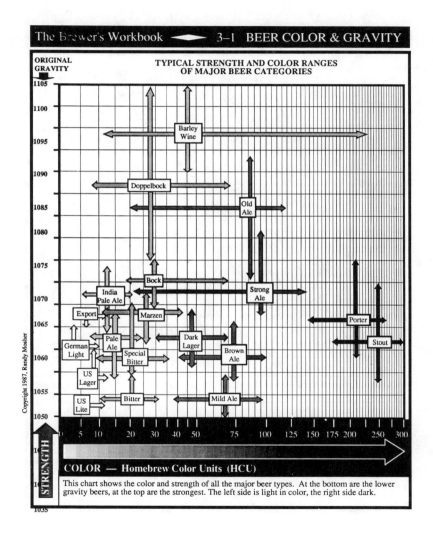

The Brewer's Workbook ➤ 3–1 BEER COLOR & GRAVITY

ORIGINAL GRAVITY

TYPICAL STRENGTH AND COLOR RANGES OF MAJOR BEER CATEGORIES

Copyright 1987, Randy Mosher

STRENGTH

COLOR — Homebrew Color Units (HCU)

This chart shows the color and strength of all the major beer types. At the bottom are the lower gravity beers, at the top are the strongest. The left side is light in color, the right side dark.

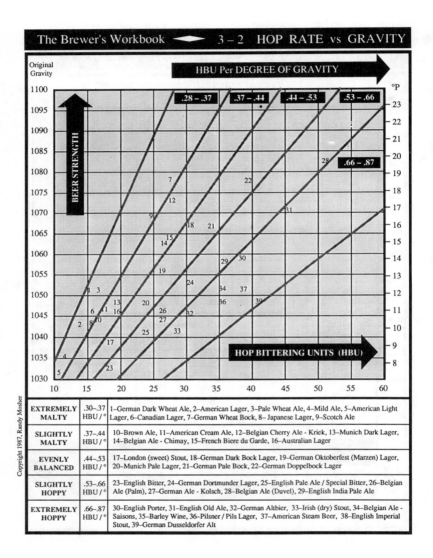

tice this, but putting it down on paper and quantifying it helps to get a handle on this very important parameter. There are a lot of variables in the use of hops, which I will talk about a little later.

Setting the Variables

When formulating the recipe, the first thing to do is to determine the specifics of the Big Three: color, gravity, and hop bitterness. If we want to brew a British bitter, we know that it should be between 15 and 35 HCUs, between 1.033 and 1.042 Original Gravity (OG), depending on whether it is a regular, best, or special bitter. For hop bitterness, somewhere between 18 and 24 HBU should be about right.

Let's make an arbitrary decision to brew in the middle of the spectrum and set our targets at 25 HCU, 1.037 OG, and 21 HBU. As we develop our recipe, these will be our goals, and we will try to find the perfect blend of ingredients to produce these characteristics. So, we need to look at the ingredients and put together a recipe.

National Style

In addition to the Big Three, there is an overlay of national style that influences the recipe in that it imposes constraints in terms of materials and techniques. Generally these follow the traditional patterns of brewing as they have developed, country by country, region by region.

Since we are brewing a bitter ale, we will be following British brewing tradition. That includes highly modified pale ale malt as the main source of extract, British varieties of hops, and the technique best suited to brewing from these materials, an infusion mash.

The Brewer's Workbook ◀— ◆ 5 – 5 1pg MASH WORKSHEET

BATCH NO		NAME			DATE		CAP
		BREWER			QTY		

DESCRIPTION

INGREDIENTS

QTY	°EXTRACT	GRAIN / ADJUNCT / SUGAR / EXTRACT	GRIND	COLOR UNITS

WATER SOURCE   CODE

WATER TREATMENT

MASH TIME & TEMP

TARGET ▶	◀ COLOR UNITS = Total Units÷Gals. ◀
ACTUAL ▶	Actual ÷ Target = Mash Efficiency ▶

QTY	HOP VARIETY		% ALPHA	TIME	UNITS

STRIKE QTY.   @   =REST

START TIME

SPARGE QTY   @ TEMP

◀ HOP BITTERING UNITS = Total Units x 17 ÷ Total Gal ◀   BOIL START   LENGTH

FERMENTATION & CONDITIONING

DATE	# DAYS	TEMP	SPECIFIC GRAVITY	% ALCOHOL / ° BALLING
			ORIGINAL GRAVITY	
			RACKING GRAVITY	
			BOTTLING GRAVITY	
			PRESSURIZED	YEAST
			CLEARED	PRIMING
			PERFECT	YIELD

% ALC ON SCALE ▼

TOTAL % ALC (Start minus end) ▼

STARTER?   DATE

NOTES

The Brewer's Workbook ◆ **5 – 5** 2 Pg **WORKSHEET**

NO.	DATE	BEER NAME		DESCRIPTION						
	QTY	BREWER								

WATER SOURCE						QTY	BOILED		STAND				

MINERAL IONS (ppm)	Ca	Mg	Na	SO₄	Cl	HCO₃	CHEMICAL	g	g/Gal	g/5Gal	ppm	I on	ppm	Ion
BEFORE TREATMENT							CaSO₄					Ca		SO₄
AFTER TREATMENT I							MgSO₄					Mg		SO₄
AFTER TREATMENT 2							NaCl					Na		Cl
TO MATCH														

QTY	°EXT 1037	GRAIN / INGREDIENT	GRIND @	COLOR @	COLOR UNITS
5		Pale Ale		5'	25
1	1006	Crystal		30	60
1/4	10015	Dark Crystal		15	45

°F / MASH START TIME / °C (temperature chart, 212°F–90°F / 100°C–30°C)

TARGET ▶ 035@	Gal	127.5 ◀ COLOR = Units /Gal
TARGET ▶	@	Gal	EFFICIENCY	% @	Gal
ACTUAL	@	Gal	EFFICIENCY	% @	Gal

(177)

QTY	HOP VARIETY	% ALPHA	TIME	UNITS
1/2	E Kent ...ikings	5	@60	2.5
3/4	" "	5	20	3.75

HRS   1   2   3   4

MASH TYPE		
TOTAL LBS	STRIKE WATER – QTY	
QT / LB	@	° = REST TEMP	TEMP DIFF
DECOC 1		DECOC 2
MASH pH	WORT pH	IRISH MOSS
BOIL START	BOIL LENGTH	CHILLER

◀ BITTER UNITS = Units x 17 / Total Gal ◀ 6.2

NOTES

We will list pale ale malt as the first ingredient in that section. We know from the extract figures published numerous places that at 100 percent mashing efficiency, one pound of pale malt per five gallons will yield 1.075 OG. We know that pale malt alone will not give us the color we need for the style of beer we are brewing, so we include some crystal malt, the lighter kind that has a color of about 80 EBC. Crystal malt yields a little less than pale, at around 1.065. A pound of crystal seems about right for this beer type, so we can go ahead and figure that in. We may also want a little of a darker crystal, to give a little more of a bite and to simplify hitting the right color. Dark crystal is in the area of about 180 EBC, so we can mark that down, too.

Personal experience has told me that in my home-brewery, I can expect about an 85 percent efficiency of mashing. That means in order to hit a gravity figure of 1.037, I need to plan for a target of 1.043.5.

The same applies to color. So to get our 25 HCU, we need to formulate for a number that is a little higher, about 29.4. To help us find the correct color, we need to know the total color units before dividing by the number of gallons. In this case, our batch is five gallons, so we just multiply that by five and get 147, which we can pencil in the box.

Now, back to the extract. We have 1.065 from the light crystal, so we need 1.037 more, which will come from the pale malt. I consult my Quick Reference Chart for Five Gallons and find that five pounds of pale ale malt will yield 1.037 degrees of gravity.

As for color, pale malt has an EBC color of 5, which gives us a figure of 25, at five pounds times five. Add that to the crystal malt already in the batch, and we get 105.

Randy Mosher

The Brewer's Workbook ◄── 5 – 2 QUICK REF – 5 Gallons

Use this chart as a handy reference for use in filling out the Brewing Worksheet when developing recipes. Make sure you use the correct version for the batch size you are brewing. The extract figures (Degrees x Pounds) are laboratory maximums, so expect to get only 85% to 95% of these, depending on your technique.

ORIGINAL GRAVITY — POUNDS, PER 5 GALLON BATCH

INGREDIENTS	1/4	1/2	1	2	3	4	5	6	7	8	9	10	11	12	13
Dextrose, Dry Malt Extract	10023	10047	10094	10188	10282	10376	10470	10564	10658	10752	10846	10940	11034	11128	11222
Malt Extract Syrup	10020	10040	10080	10160	10246	10320	10400	10480	10560	10640	10720	10800	10880	10960	11040
Corn, Rice	10019	10039	10079	10158	10237	10316	10395	10474	10553	10632	10711	10790	10869	10948	11027
Wheat Malt	10019	10039	10078	10156	10234	10312	10390	10468	10546	10624	10702	10780	10858	10936	11014
English 2-Row Lager,Pale	10018	10037	10075	10150	10225	10300	10375	10450	10525	10600	10675	10750	10825	10900	10975
English Mild Ale Malt,	10018	10036	10072	10144	10216	10288	10360	10432	10504	10576	10648	10720	10792	10864	10936
German 2-Row Pilsner Malt	10017	10035	10070	10140	10210	10280	10350	10420	10490	10560	10630	10700	10770	10840	10910
German 2-Row Munich Malt	10017	10034	10069	10138	10207	10276	10345	10414	10483	10552	10621	10690	10759	10828	10897
Light Crystal, Dextrine Malt	10016	10032	10065	10130	10195	10260	10325	10390	10455	10520	10585	10650	10715	10780	10845
Brown, Amber Malt	10016	10032	10064	10128	10192	10256	10320	10384	10448	10512	10576	10640	10704	10768	10832
US, Canadian 6-Row Lager	10015	10031	10063	10126	10186	10248	10310	10372	10434	10496	10558	10620	10682	10744	10806
ChocolateMalt, Dk Crystal	10015	10030	10061	10122	10183	10244	10305	10366	10427	10488	10549	10610	10671	10732	10793
Black Malt, Roast Barley	10015	10030	10060	10120	10180	10240	10300	10360	10420	10480	10540	10600	10660	10720	10780

HOP ALPHA ACID % — Use to calculate bitterness level of finished beer.

VARIETY	% Alpha	VARIETY	%Alpha	VARIETY	% Alpha
Brewer's Gold	7 – 10	Fuggles	4 – 7	Perle	7 – 9
Bullion	7 – 10	Galena	12 – 14	Olympic	12 – 14
Cascade	5 – 7	Golding	3.5 – 5	Saaz	4 – 8
Chinook	12 – 14	Hallertau	4 – 8	Styrian Goldings	6 – 8.5
Cluster	7 – 9	Hersbrucker	3 – 6	Spalt	6 – 8
Colombia	8 – 10	Kent Golding	5 – 7	Talisman	7 – 9
Comet	8 – 10	N. Brewer	7 – 10	Tettnanger	4 – 6
Eroica	11 – 13	Nugget	12 – 14	Willamette	6 – 8

GRAIN COLOR

INGREDIENT	COLOR UNITS
Corn, Rice	0
Pilsner, Lager	2
Pale Ale	5
Mild Ale	7.5
Munich	8.5
Wheat Malt	16
Amber	60
Light Crystal	85
Brown	160
Dark Crystal	190
Chocolate	1000
Roast Barley	1200
Blk. Patent Malt	1350

SUGAR WT./ VOLUME

CUPS =	Oz	Gm
1 Tbsp	0.43	13
1/8 Cup	0.84	23.7
1/4 Cup	1.67	47.3
1/3 Cup	2.23	63.2
3/8 Cup	2.50	71.0
1/2 Cup	3.34	94.7
5/8 Cup	4.16	118
2/3 Cup	4.45	126
3/4 Cup	5.01	142
7/8 Cup	5.84	166
1 Cup	6.68	189
1 1/4 Cup	8.35	237
1 1/2 Cup	10.0	284

HOP BITTERING UNITS

Multiply alpha acid % by number of ounces, add up total, then multiply by 3.14, for 5 gallon batch size.

HOMEBREW COLOR

Multiply grain color by number of pounds, add up total, then divide by number of gallons to get Homebrew Color Units.

PRIMING RATES

ALE— Lt. 1.0 oz/gal
       Med. 1.15 oz/gal
LAGER –Lt. 1.45 oz/gal
       Med. 1.6 oz/gal

°F / °C scale

210–100, 200–95, 190–90, 180–85, 170–80, 160–75, 150–70, 140–65, 130–60, 120–55, 110–50, 100–45, 90–40/35, 80–30/25, 70–20, 60

O.G. / °PLATO scale

1120–28, 1115–27, 1110–26, 1105–25, 1100–23, 1095–22, 1090–21, 1085–20, 1080–18, 1075–17, 1070–16, 1065–14, 1060–13, 1055–11, 1050–10, 1045–9, 1040–8, 1035–7, 1030–6, 1025–5, 1020–4, 1015–3, 1010–2, 1005–1, 1000–0

OZ / GRAMS scale

3.4–100, 3.2–90, 3.0–85, 2.8–80/75, 2.6–70, 2.4–65, 2.2–60, 2.0–50, 1.8–45, 1.6–40, 1.4–35, 1.2–30, 1.0–25, 0.8–20, 0.6–15, 0.4–10, 0.2–5, 0.0–0

Subtract that from the 147 target color, and that leaves us with 42 more units of color to be added. The simplest thing to do is to just get it from the dark crystal. We can add enough to get the color we want without adding a great deal to the gravity. And 42 divided by 180 gives 0.23, or about a quarter pound.

To just clean up the numbers, let's figure a real quarter pound, which would give us 45 color units. Add up all the color, and we get 150. Multiply it times our expected yield of 85 percent and we get 127.5. Divide that by five, and we get the HCUs for this beer, which at 25.5 is close to the beginning specs. Obviously you can spend more time and fine-tune this process to arrive at exactly the numbers you want.

To sum up the gravity, we have 1.037 from the pale malt, 1.006 from the light crystal, 1.001 from the dark crystal, which gives us a total target figure of 1.045. Multiply that by 85 percent and the result is 1.038, in the neighborhood for a best bitter. We could pull out a quarter to a half a pound of pale malt, and we would hit it right on the head.

Malt extract, dry or syrup, can be figured exactly the same way. Calculating color is a little trickier, since most manufacturers don't release color figures. You just have to trust them when they say a beer is a certain type. The one thing to remember is that most of them formulate color for a single can of extract per recipe. The rest of the extract comes from sugar, which contributes no color to the brew. So if you use more than one can of extract, your beer will be twice as dark as it should be. There is not much

Fred Eckhardt, beer author and long-time homebrewer, is the first recipient of the American Homebrewers Association's Recognition Award for his outstanding contributions to the homebrewing community. Presenting the award is Charlie Papazian.

you can do about the lighter beers, but for the medium and darker beers, just make the second can a lighter color rather than the dark.

Grain Grind

If you are grinding your own grain for mashing, there can be quite a lot of variation in the efficiency of your mash, depending on the fineness or coarseness of your grind. One column in the grain record simply allows you to track this. My grinder is a worn-out, old, grocery-store coffee mill, and I have put a piece of white tape along the adjusting knob and marked it into divisions numbered 1 to 10. Having that information helped me determine the best grind to get the maximum extract from my malt. I think you could do that kind of calibration with a Corona mill or whatever you are using.

Hop Bitterness

Figuring the hop rate is much the same, except that I have used a factor that takes the familiar HBUs and allows them to be converted to IHBUs, the ppm measurement of isomerized hop alpha acids. Using the HBU conversion factor is worth doing, as it allows any of us to compare our products to commercially brewed beers, for which there is plenty of published data. Professional brewers usually use a number of about 22.5 , which assumes a 30 percent rate of incorporation of alpha acids into finished beer. I feel this is a little high, so here I have used a number of 17, which corresponds to a 23 percent utilization rate. This is one area where there can be enormous variation from one brew to the next, and it is very difficult to nail down exactly. At this time, there is no accepted homebrew standard for this conversion factor.

Having set the bitterness target for 21 HBU, the first thing is to convert that back to ounces-times-alpha acid (AA) percentage. To do that, we multiply the HBU target by the number of gallons (5), then divide by the HBU conversion factor (17). That gives us 6.2 as a figure to shoot at — the alpha acid percentage times the quantity in ounces of hops present. That means we can have one ounce of hops at 6.2 percent AA, or half an ounce of hops at 13.4 percent AA, or any other combination that will add up to the number 6.2. This, of course, is for the bittering hops only. I include any hops boiled twenty minutes or more, that time limit being somewhat of an arbitrary cut-off. Shorter boils decrease hop incorporation rates, but it gets pretty complicated trying to calculate all that. This is supposed to be a hobby, right? So, the hop boil length is just one more item on our long list of "fudge factors."

Since we are making an English ale, we should use English-style hops. Goldings are the traditional hops of choice for Pale ales. Let's assume we have some nice, fresh East Kent Goldings with an alpha acid content of 5.0. To reach that 6.2 figure, we can use 1.25 ounces total (6.2 divided 5 equals 1.24). I would use .50 ounce during the whole boil, and .75 ounce for the last twenty minutes, putting the emphasis on the aromatic side.

If you are using different hop types with varying AA percentages, split the target (ounces times AA percentage), and assign part of this number to each of the hop types being used. Then figure each type separately. For example, you could assign .33 of this, or 2.0, to a high-alpha hop such as Chinook. The rest, 4.4, could then be derived from the East Kent Goldings. There is no numerical magic to the aromatic hops added. Just do what you usually do and be sure to mark it down in the hop section of the brewing work sheet.

Water Chemistry

This can really get quite complicated, so I'm not going to try to cover it here in much detail. I use one section to record the specifics of water treatment I may have used on any given batch. First I record the source of water I am brewing with and list its raw, untreated mineral analysis. This may be obtained by writing to the local water company. The important ions for brewing are Calcium, Magnesium, Sodium, Sulfate, Chloride, and Bicarbonate.

I also list the minerals in the water I am trying to match. I record the results of the first treatment, which for me is usually subtractive — removing the bulk of the carbonate ions by boiling and decanting the water prior to brewing. On the next line, I usually list additive treatment. This may seem like a tedious process, but remember that you won't have to do this too many times, unless you are brewing with a different water type for every batch of beer.

Fudge Factors

While we are still in the recipe section of the worksheet, I would like to talk about what I call "fudge factors." These are variables best guessed at rather than calculated, at least in homebrewing. Brewing has numerous materials and processes that can cause your beer to depart from the expected values as calculated. Here are some of the more important ones.

Grain Fudge Factors

Wort gravity can depart from what is expected for many reasons. For one, grains vary from year to year, which causes variation in the mashing process. I got a 10 percent improvement in yield simply by adjusting the grind of my grain. When you are mashing, the total amount of wort sparged and the total volume boiled can vary from batch to batch. Gravity is an area that is easily adjusted by adding a little dry extract or diluting the wort or the finished beer to get exactly the starting gravity you want. Fortunately, most beer categories have a lot of lattitude in this regard.

Surprisingly, water minerals can have an effect on the color of beer. Water high in carbonate, or temporary hardness, can impart a reddish cast that is considered inappropriate for pale beers. This is one reason why high-carbonate water has traditionally been reserved for the production of darker beers, such as Munich dark and brown ales.

Finally, it is difficult to produce a really pale beer, given the fire-brewing habits of almost all homebrewers. The intense localized heat of the flame may create some caramelization of the sugars in the wort, resulting in a dark beer. This is really only noticeable in pale in pale and light amber beers.

Hop Fudge Factors

This is the biggest and trickiest group of variables in brewing:

1) Whole hops are less bitter than pellets.
2) Storage affects bitterness somewhat, but not as much as you might think.
3) Water chemistry. High carbonate water brings out a harsh hop bitterness that makes beers seem more bitter.
4) Wort strength. Hop incorporation decreases as wort gravity increases. This is part of the reason for the ridiculously high hopping rates on barley wines.
5) In determining duration of fermentation, bitterness of beer decreases with time. It seems to me to lose about half of its bitterness in six months or so. This is another reason for high bitterness rates in strong beers.
6) The length and vigor of boil introduce variability to the calculated bitterness.
7) Real vs. estimated alpha acid content. If you are using hops without a pedigree, an alpha acid percentage determined by analysis, you could be off by as much as 50 percent. There is often considerable variation from one

year to the next, and of course, those variations are passed along to your beer.

Dealing with Fudge Factors

These little details can make you crazy if you let them. While a great deal of attention, is paid to them by commercial breweries, for us homebrewers they are best left unquantified. No one expects a certain type of wine to taste the same every year. Variation is part of the fun and the quest of fine wines, and there is no reason it should be any different for fine beers.

Just consider the fudge factors when you set your targets and make allowances for them. If, for example, you are brewing a strong beer that will age for may months, raise the HBU target. If you are brewing exclusively with pellets, lower it a bit. Those are the kinds of things you accommodate. Simply use common sense. If there are things out of your control, like an unknown hop AA percentage, relax. Aim for the middle and get on with it.

In terms of homebrewers jargon: Relax, don't worry, have a homebrew. Or, relax, worry just a little, have enough homebrew so that you don't worry too much.

Brewing Process Information

Let's move onto tracking the brewing process itself.

I have created four different worksheets designed to be used for various brewing levels. The one I am showing here, the Non-Mash Worksheet, is a very simple sheet I use for new brewers. It includes just the basics, which is plenty for some people. Names, dates, ingredients, minimal water treatment, ingredients, boiling data, and a section to track the fermentation of the brew as it

Randy Mosher

The Brewer's Workbook ◆ 5-4 NON-MASH WORKSHEET

BATCH NO	NAME		DATE		CAP
	BREWER		QTY		

DESCRIPTION

INGREDIENTS

QTY	°EXTRACT	EXTRACT / SUGAR / ETC.	BITTER UNITS	COLOR UNITS	WATER SOURCE — CODE
					BOILED
					GYPSUM ADDED
					EPSOM SALTS ADDED
					OTHER TREATMENT
					OTHER INGREDIENTS

TARGET ▶   ◀ COLOR UNITS = Total Units ÷ Gals. ◀

QTY	HOP VARIETY	% ALPHA	TIME	UNITS	
					QTY WORT BOILED
					BOIL LENGTH
					IRISH MOSS?
					WORT CHILLER?
					QTY AT PRIMARY
					QTY AT SECONDARY
	BITTERNESS FROM EXTRACTS		—		CHAOS FACTOR

◀ HOP BITTERING UNITS = Total Units x 17 ÷ Total Gal ◀

FERMENTATION & CONDITIONING	% ALCOHOL	0 1 2 3 4 5 6 · 7 8 9 10 11 12 13	% ALC ON SCALE ▼	TOTAL % ALC
	° BALLING	0 1 2 3 4 5 6 7 8 9 10 11 12 13 14 15 16 17 18 19 20 21 22 23		(Start minus end) ▼

DATE	# DAYS	TEMP	SPECIFIC GRAVITY	1010 1020 1030 1040 1050 1060 1070 080 1090
			ORIGINAL GRAVITY	
			RACKING GRAVITY	
			BOTTLING GRAVITY	
			PRESSURIZED	YEAST STARTER? DATE
			CLEARED	PRIMING
			PERFECT	YIELD

NOTES

progresses from wort to primary to secondary, and finally, to finished beer.

The two little scales show degrees Balling, and more importantly, percentage of potential alcohol. Just draw a line from the original gravity scale up to the % Alcohol scale and record that number at the right. When the beer is bottled, do the same thing. Then subtract the second reading from the first and mark it down. There is room for information on priming materials and quantities, as well as final yield of the batch.

The One-Page Mash Worksheet has room for more detailed data and can be used for mashed batches, although it can be a little cramped for that. It is quite adequate for mini-mashes, though.

The third sheet is the Two-Page Worksheet pictured earlier. It includes most everything any serious homebrewer would want.

For people like myself, who have really gone off the deep end, there is the Four-Page version. It is pretty much like the two-page sheet, with water treatment and a mash chart, but it provides lots of room for long ingredient lists and fine divisions on the mashing time-and-temperature chart.

I made one page for "During the Brew," which includes space for information about strike water quantities and temperatures. These are useful to track as it is important to use the right amount of water at a specific temperature to get the mash stabilized at the correct temperature. Recording this information will allow you to fine-tune the process over the period of a few batches, ultimately making your brewing better and even more painless.

Gil Ortega, brewmaster at Coors Pilot Brewery, judges homebrew in the National HomebrewCompetition.

The Mash Chart is simply a record of time and temperatures of the mashing process as it progresses. I usually check the temperature every fifteen minutes or so. I draw a line on the chart in pencil before I begin and use that as a guide line during mashing. I record the actual mash temperature with a pen as I go along. I use a solid line for the mash itself and a dashed line for decoctions or adjunct mashes. I also list detailed information on decoctions. This is important for the same reason as strike water is.

The third page has three sections identical to the fermentation section on the other worksheets. But it also allows me to split the main batch into three individual batches, which may be treated separately. Different yeast, fermentation temperatures, even additives such as fruit are possible. It is really handy with larger batch sizes.

The last page of the four-pager is this evaluation sheet. Like the fermentation section, it is divided into three batches. The beer can be evaluated for various sensory qualities and judged against an ideal for the type. The categories are a simplified version of the ones used by independent testing labs such as the Siebel Institute. It simply imposes some discipline on the process. What you should arrive at with a form like this is a listing of changes you would make for the next version of the same beer—more bitter, less dark, things like that.

In addition to the central brewing log, there are other sheets that are useful in other aspects of the home-brew process. One is the Water Correction Worksheet. Another is the Recipe Worksheets. These are simplified versions of the brewing worksheets and can be used for fiddling around with recipes without wasting a whole log sheet. The Brew Summary holds the vital statistics of your brews so you can line them up and compare them. This is handy for hanging up in your cellar for a quick reference on the beers available for drinking. It is really useful if you have friends you trade your beer with.

The beer is not the only thing you will want to keep track of. Ingredients, especially hops, have variations that can affect beer flavor. I use a Hop Data Worksheet to list the quantities and alpha acid percentages of the hops I buy. You can even track your hop inventory as you brew.

Beyond the ingredients is the fermenting environment, and I use the Brewery Temperature Log to track this. I simply post it in my conditioning cellar and write down the temperature from time to time. I placed two or three in different parts of my basement.

Summary

I hope this doesn't sound like a tremendous amount of work because it really isn't. The most difficult part is the number crunching of recipe formulation— getting intimate with a pocket calculator. But it does pay the greatest rewards—consistent, delicious beer that is exactly what you had in mind when you set out to brew. The other areas are more a matter of structured note-taking, and really, this is easier than trying to write it all down on a blank sheet of paper.

I keep all the sheets in a three ring binder, my master brewing book. I keep the most recently brewed recipes at the very front for easy access, then older brews. Then I have a divider and a section full of untried recipes. After that comes reference material and other log sheets like the ones on water and hops. In the back is a supply of blank worksheets of different varieties.

Randy Mosher is a long-time, successful home-brewer with a gift for organization of the brewing process. The worksheets presented here are from his forthcoming book, The Brewer's Workbook.

Participant points out the qualities of a good beer.

7.
Bavarian Breweries

Prince Luitpold von Bayern
Kaltenberg Brewery

It may be strange to you that a Bavarian Prince is speaking about beer. In England, people say, "There is beerage and peerage." If you were to visit Bavaria, you would find that life is different than it is here, and there is a completely different attitude toward beer. We have the saying that beer is the fifth element of a Bavarian citizen. It is the centerpiece of people's daily life. At beerfests, we have big beer festivals and all the people from the neighborhoods come — two or three thousand people. We go into a beer tent and have a little church service with a brass band playing church music. Once the service is finished, the keg is tapped and the party begins. This is an example that explains our attitude toward beer.

In my case there is a very strong tie with my family and beer. My family, the House of Wittelsbach, ruled Bavaria from 1180 until 1918, which makes it the longest ruling family in Europe. Very early my ancestors were into brewing. Our first brewery dates back to 1260 when Duke

Ludwig the Severe moved his residence from Landshut to
Munich. The brewery can be traced to the early 1400s, but
it is very difficult to find many details about it because the
archives in Munich burned in late 1400.

Later, our family always had breweries, mainly in
castles such as Nympenburg, Hohenschwargen, Schlei-
shein. In researching I located references to nearly seventy breweries. We also very early got into legislation
about beer. One of my ancestors, Wilhelm IV, made the
famous Reinheitsgebot Purity Law, a law that was the
most significant in beer brewing. It is the oldest food
control law in Europe, perhaps in all the world, and is still
valid today. It decreed that beer was to be made from hops,
water, malt, and yeast, and no other additives. The reason
for doing this was to protect consumers and for consumer
assurance. Brewers at that time were adding many different things to their beers, and the law was instituted to
make beer what it is today — a pure and clean drink.

In 1570 our family was very lucky to get the
monopoly in the production of Weissbier. There was only
one brewery in Bavaria brewing this special beer, and our
family acquired it. We had the monopoly for producing
Weissbier in Bavaria for nearly two hundred years. In
fact, it provided the biggest income for the Bavarian dukes
and provided them with the cash to fight the Thirty Year
War. Without our production of Weissbier, there wouldn't
be any Catholics left in Europe.

Besides brewing, our family members, along with
other Bavarian citizens, were keen consumers of beer. We
have exact records in our family archives about the daily
consumption of food and beverage in the Bavarian court in
1650, which included perhaps two hundred people eating

lunch and dinner. The archives list, by name, who ate and drank how much. From 1650 to about 1800, we have the daily consumption of the Bavarian rulers, of the Father of Confession, of the ladies of the court. The Duke Elektor Max Emanuel, for example, always drank a liter of beer for lunch and a liter of beer for dinner, whereas his son had a liter of beer for lunch and half a bottle of Burgundy for dinner. The Father of Confession had more than two liters of beer per day. One can say from these statistics that the consumption of beer was fairly constant and that beer was consumed by the rulers and not only by the blue collar workers. Everyone drank beer as one of their most important items of food.

Today, this habit continues. The per head consumption of Bavarian citizens is 220 liters per annum, which is by far the highest in the world. Beer comprises 20 percent of what the average person spends on food and is the highest portion by volume of people's intake of food. It also is a very important part of our economy. We are a nation of microbrewers. At this time, we have 780 breweries operating in Bavaria, and they produce 25 million hectoliters, an average of 32,400 hectoliters per brewery.

In Germany, in total are 1,161 microbrewers producing an average of 79,000 hectoliters. You can see that Northern Germany has larger breweries than Southern Germany (Bavaria). According to these statistics, Bavaria has one of every four breweries in the world, which is remarkable for a small country. All of these breweries have a variety of vital products. We believe that we have approximately 5,000 different labels of beer in German with a wide range of different styles, all brewed to the Reinheitsgebot.

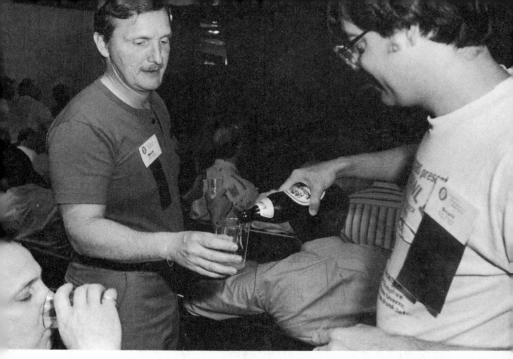

Prince Luitpold's gift to conference participants, Prinzregent Luitpold Weissbier from Kaltenberg Brewery, was sampled and appreciated.

You may know that the Reinheitsgebot came under severe pressure in the European common market. There are two sides to this issue. In Germany, what the court case on the Reinheitsgebot means is that:

1. German beer will continue to be made to the Reinheitsgebot, the result of which is that it doesn't change our industry;

2. Other alcoholic malt and grain beverages may be sold in Germany, which was also true in the past. We have never banned other malt and grain beverages. The only thing we disallowed was for them to be called "beer." Now Germany is obliged to let these products in under the name of beer, but we have the option through the German Minister of Health to define how the declaration on the labels must read. At this time, German brewers are fighting that the delaration shouldn't just be on the label

but should also be on the menu cards of the bar. If it were not, a customer might order a beer from the menu card and get a product made out of potatoes, corn , fish bladders, who knows what? So we are asking for a list of the ingredients in the products.

The German Minister of Health also has the prerogative to ban certain additives in beer, in particular formaldehyde, which is commonly used in France and Denmark. I don't believe we should ingest what medical men generally use to preserve corpses.

The result is that there is basically no problem with the Reinheitsgebot for German beers. In that regard, Germany hasn't lost the court case but has won it because people in other European countries are starting to question quite loudly the reason why aren't our beers allowed into Germany? The controversy definitely has drawn a great deal of attention to the high quality of our beers. I think that in a time when people are worried about things like Chernobyl, pollution, and additives, purity should be a big concern and the main word in labeling. Maybe brewers can produce a very tasty product brewed with additives, but it isn't good for the industry. For the industry, we need consumers who believe in beer—consumers who think it is clean and accept it not as an alcoholic beverage but as a clean, pure, food product. I think you should introduce the Reinheitsgebot into North America, which would draw people's attention to that purity.

I would like to speak about our own breweries, the Kaltenberg Brewery. One can imagine that in a market such as Germany's, where there are so many breweries, there is a very soft margin. It is a market where one has to be very, very careful what one does or one won't survive

Some of the microbrewers who participated in the Great American Beer Festival.

for long. Our brewery is, for German standards, above average although we aren't very big. We are running three different breweries. We have one that specializes mainly in dark beer, one specializing mainly in top-fermenting beers, and one doing the other beers and distribution. In those breweries, we produce a wide range of beer,.

Over the last ten years, we have had continuing growth at a very sound rate. My greatest attention has always been to quality and credibility. I believe that beer is a product that doesn't forgive mistakes. One has to be aware of that. A lot of people need to have much more concern about their quality. If not, it creates a dangerous situation. Once your reputation suffers, it is very hard to stay in business. A brewer has to believe that the product he is producing is authentic. The consumer doesn't want to be fooled. If a brewer disappoints him, it will reflect on the entire industry as he will doubt every brewery product. We have worked very strongly on quality and have built up quality control. We were very small ten years ago, but by trying to have consistent products—products with characteristics of each type of beer, we started to build up a reputation for very good quality. Now we have a certain edge on our competitors.

We also depend a lot on blind tasting. One has to admit that most brewmasters are not fair to their own product. They have produced it, and they don't want to admit it if they have made a mistake. So all brewmasters should do more blind tasting and let other people judge their beers. We do blind tastings in our own company, but we also let our beers be tasted by other people on a monthly basis to see whether or not we are doing well. This includes tastings at the Bavarian Brewing University. The problem is that if a consumer doesn't like a brewer's beer, he won't tell the brewer; he simply won't come back. Particularly in a brewpub, customers don't say, "Your beer is no good." But they will not return.

We produce a number of specialty beers. In our region around Munich, we have a full range of beers including Helles, or light beer, seasonal beers, special beers, three types of Weissbier, Dunkle, Pils, and a lot of dark beer. A brewer should never forget the fact that making and drinking a beer should invite the consumer to drink one more. If the brewer can achieve that, then he has been a good brewer. If people want to stop at one beer, then he has done something wrong. One key is to make sure that the character of the beer is not exaggerated just to make it "different." To achieve a perfect beer is long, intensive work with continuous refinement on the product.

At Kaltenberg, we have specialized in two products: Konig Ludwig Dunkel and Prinzregent Luitpold Weissbier. We are the leader in Bavaria with Dunkle. Our Weissbier has the best pedigree in our industry, and we are growing faster than our competition. We worked for years and years to improve one of our Dunkle beers. One of the biggest challenges was to produce a dark lager with no bitterness of black malt. That is hard work if you don't want to use colored beer. Our Weissbier is a very old-fashioned beer and one that shouldn't have any off flavor. We usually have a lot of yeast in our finished beer. The reason is that when you drink our beer, you get the Vitamin B12. People go to the pharmacy and buy Brewer's Yeast in a health or beauty kit, but we sell it in the sediment of the bottle.

Internationally, we have the philosophy of cooperating with brewers We have production in Sweden, in England, and by the end of 1988, we are going to launch our beers in two other European countries. This licensed production has forced us to do extensive work on our techniques, particularly in the pure breeding of yeast and in quality control. We also established a technical unit capable of controlling our production. When we went into manufacturing mini-breweries, from the technical side, to licensing control, to yeast shipment was pure synergy.

The way we got started with minibreweries was that some years ago, I visited a brewpub in England and was fascinated by the idea of a pubbrewery for two reasons. One was that I have been fighting a battle for years with the town of Munich because it allows only Munich

breweries to serve at the Oktoberfest. Originally, Oktoberfest was a wedding party for my great-grandfather and
he held the first Oktoberfest. Now our brewery is slightly
out of town, and so we cannot get into Oktoberfest. My goal
became to buy a brewery and put it in a tent at Oktoberfest. To make a long story short, Munich changed the
rules, and I still did not get in, even after a long year's
battle .

Once I had the pubbrewery, we began experimenting and refining our products. After a few years of experimentation, we thought it would be nice to start running
many breweries. We had a good reputation for our bottled
beer, and we went to the Eastern Bloc, where there are
cooperatives. We went into a joint venture and put a
pubbrewery into Budapest to see what would happen.
Beer has basically five enemies: light, oxygen, temperature changes, shaking, and time. But in a pubbrewery,
none of those apply. A brewpub always has fresh beer,
which is the best beer for the consumer. The beer isn't
exposed to any of the hazards, and it can be very good,
provided it is brewed with the same high standards for
quality and consistency as a big brewery has.

The brewery in Budapest proved to be a fantastic
success. It has been packed since the day it opened in
October 1985. We found that this was an area where we
could apply our synergetic efforts for a brewing company.
We were able to make use of all our expertise to control
license production. We could supply software to pubbreweries from defining and controlling raw materials such as
malt to defining quality control standards. We could
supply and ship yeast, and we could supply personnel and
train them in our pubbrewery.

Husband and wife Homebrewers of the Year, Nancy Vineyard (1983) and Byron Burch (1986), listen to Prince Luitpold's description of brewpubs near Munich.

The next step was to contribute our own equipment. We have set up a company doing turn-key brewpubs. In June 1986, we delivered the first brewpubs of our own equipment into Hungry, which proved to be another big success. We have sold another ten since then, and by the end of 1988, we will have sixteen of them in operation in Hungary as a franchiseable chain. All are produced under the trade name HBH, Haus Brau Hof.

In March 1987, we opened the first one in Germany in Stuttgart. This one has sold close to 3,000 barrels in a year doing one product only, which is sold in 0.2 liter glasses. The brewpub has made a net profit of $2 million in one year. This brewpub didn't aim at low price. Its beer is the most expensive in Stuttgart. The brewpub sells only one beer, coffee, mineral water, apple juice, and one kind of schapps. It is a beautiful, clean concept that has proven to be very successful.

We have five brewpubs in Germany now, and one in Italy. We have put a brewery in downtown Munich that is producing two products for the purpose of training brewers for our pubbreweries. We are going to brew both top- and bottom-fermenting beers to teach people how to brew these styles. All of these, with the exception of the one in Stuttgart, have a service contract so we can provide weekly quality control. We feel that if a pubbrewery doesn't have sufficient quality control, it will end up with product failure sooner or later. Normally, the brewer will detect it too late.

Tight quality control is crucial, and I believe that we have many possibilities of learning from big breweries that are friendly to small breweries. Why shouldn't there be a good relationship between the large and the small? It doesn't harm them, and it is a good opportunity for us to build a more solid reputation.

So far it seems that a good future lies ahead for pubbreweries. I do have doubts about the wisdom of going from a pubbrewery to a microbrewery with a bottling line. My reserve towards this comes from the fact that as soon as a brewer gets into bottled products, he is fighting all the problems big breweries have. Shelf-life, product consistency, labor relations, and problems with brewery reputation are bound to result. Yet, if a brewer has a good pubbrewery, he has all the margins to make a lot more money. For one thing, customers have to go to the establishment to get the beer. This enables the brewer to charge more.

I don't believe the step from pubbrewery to microbrewery is inevitable. I don't believe a brewer needs all the headaches of packaged products. I believe that big breweries will always be better at that, and as soon as a brewery is successful, it will run the risk of being overtaken. Big breweries will sooner or later realize the danger of small package plants, but against pubbreweries, they will have no argument because the brewery is selling freshness. That is a concept they can't do.

Prince Luitpold of Bavaria is the owner of Kaltenberg Brewery, which dates to the Thirteenth Century and is located in a Bavarian castle outside Munich. Luitpold has provided consulting services to many persons starting brewpubs in Europe, as well as working in joint venture with persons opening pubbreweries of his design.

Gold Medal winner Geoffrey Larson takes the first step back to Alaska.

8.
Making Amazing Mead

Leon Havill
Havill's Mazer Mead Company

I would like to tell you a little about the mead we make at our place in Rangiora, New Zealand. My wife Gay is here with me, and if it weren't for her help and assistance over the years, I am quite sure that we wouldn't be as far ahead as we are today. She has had to put up with lots of awful things. I am the one who is inclined to leap into things, but she is the steadying influence coming along saying, "Come on, now. Just do things quietly." If it weren't for her, I think I would have gone off the track years ago.

How many of you are mead makers? The rest of you just look around at those who are holding up their hands; they are the picture of health and well-being. I could actually have picked them out from where I am standing up here. Some poor folks don't know what mead is. In my opinion, a true, or traditional, mead is made from fermented honey. It contains no fruit, vegetables, herbs,

spices, preservatives, or hangovers. You don't get a hangover from mead, you know. I had one young fellow who came into my place and said that he had a hangover from the mead. I questioned him about it and he said, "Well, it wasn't much of a hangover. But I drank three bottles before I got home, and then two more when I arrived." I told him, "Well, look, we're here for the mead and not the greed."

The reason you don't get a hangover from mead is that it is not an acid fermentation. So I am told, you can get several undesirable compounds being formed in an acid fermentation, one of them being ether. Ether used to be distilled from fruit-based wines and used as anaesethetic. If you are old enough to remember being put down with ether, you probably remember the nasty aftereffect of a hangover that went on for days. What ether they used to have left over from the operations, they used for running racing cars. So if you want to marinate your brain, drink some fruit-based wine.

The first reference to mead in history appears in a cave drawing in Spain. It was drawn between twelve and fourteen thousand years ago, and depicted several people up a ladder gathering honey. The only reason we know they are gathering honey is that whoever drew the picture had enough sense to draw a few king-size bees zooming around the gatherers' heads. If ever this picture is used in a history book or a beekeeping journal, they always cut it off two rungs below the gatherers' feet. What our ancestors were getting to at the bottom of the ladder has to do with the honey's and the mead's reputed aphrodisiac qualities, and is certainly not fit for family viewing.

Getting a little nearer our time, in India in the

I said, "Yes."

"Well, there is honey all through the telephone book. Have you been in the sitting room, too?"

I said, "Yes."

"It's all over the sofa, too," she said. "Look, Dear, I really think you should shift this out to the shed."

That wasn't exactly what she said, but it was what she meant.

I moved my brewing to the shed, and we brewed away. Some brews were good, some were terrible, but of course, we didn't know what mead should taste like. That was a little problem! I belong to a dance band, and my friends in the band are all beer drinkers. So everytime we went out to play somewhere, I would bring a few bottles of my latest brew and try it on the boys in the band. I have been doing that now for over twenty years, and they are still good friends. Sometimes they were very ruthless. If they didn't like it, they told me. But they did like some brews, and I thought that if it appealed to beer drinkers, I couldn't go too far wrong from a commercial point of view.

You have to realize that our country has a population of only 75 million—sheep, that is. Only 3 million people. Someone said that New Zealand is like a poultry farm that hasn't had a new rooster for 100 years. He may be right.

We live on the South Island, and Christchurch, our main city, has 600,000 people. Our local town has 6,000. Two-thirds of the population, or 2 million people, live at the top end of the North Island some 1,500 miles away. So we had to make something that was going to appeal to a lot of people. We couldn't afford to risk starting into the business without having something that would be marketable.

Greg Giorgio contemplates the reputed powers of mead. According to mead-maker Leon Havill, next to Heaven, Rangiora, New Zealand, is the most likely place to find good mead.

The recipe I gave was the one we used for thirteen years, although we did alter it 850 times before we could get a brew that had an acceptable taste and also fermented out fairly quickly. A lot of the brews were taking up to two years to ferment, and after some time, we got it down to the place where we could ferment a brew in six months. While we were brewing, we also were trying to get the law changed. The law said that wine could be made out of fruits, vegetables, or grapes, so one had to be registered as a fruit winemaker or a grape winemaker. Honey had no category, and we couldn't get a license. We pedaled that through the courts for ten years before we got the law changed and were allowed to sell mead.

I was ecstatic when the law passed. We had a bookshop at the time, and we decided to sell it right away and get brewing. Well, ten years later, we still had the shop. Gay was keeping the income coming in at the shop, looking after the family, looking after the housework, and I was building a meadery. We started in half-gallon jars, and escalated to forty-gallon barrels, then to 100-gallon tanks, then to 200-gallon tanks, and to 400-gallon tanks. But despite the size of the tanks, we did all our experimenting in half-gallon jars. I remember when we first brewed in the 200-gallon tanks, and the mead fermentation just stopped dead. I rushed off and called an old friend who was a winemaker. He looked in the tank, took a few samples out, and told me the yeast was sour.

"You have to feed the yeast," he said.

He added some various things and came back about a fortnight later. He went over to the tank, lifted the lid, looked in, shouted, "Jesus Christ," and slammed down the lid. I had a look and the whole tank had gone solid. We literally had to shovel the slimy mess out of the tank into the garden. Well, that one cost a couple thousand dollars.

I decided to try another way of solving the problem. Red Star yeast was involved in that. My friend pitched it in, came back a couple of weeks later, and we had the most awful brew of something like acetone. It was not thickening any, so we pumped it out under the trees and it was the greatest weed killer you ever saw in your life. The grass was burned off, and not a blade of grass came up for eighteen months.

My friend slunk off saying, "I think I'll leave you to your Medieval beer."

But finally, we got the process down pat, and today we have the brews coming through relatively quickly. The best one I had was in nine days, 14 percent by volume alcohol. The slower ones are taking from twenty-one to twenty-eight days.

At that stage, we began getting out first customers. I had been scouring the countryside trying to find someone who could tell me about mead. A group of senior citizens— all in their eighties—came to the meadery. They got off the bus, coming up the drive with their little bags in one hand, and their walking sticks in the other. I gave them a few glasses of mead, and you wouldn't believe the difference. They were running down the driveway to the bus, shouting and singing. The bus driver said they were the best group he had ever had. They sang almost all the way back to the city, and then they went to sleep.

I cleaned up the driveway after they left and found a lot of discarded walking sticks along the way. I took them to the hospital, of course, to donate them to people who hadn't had mead. Eventually, our place began to become known as the "Lourdes of the South Pacific." I know that you will agree that that trail of walking sticks was a miracle. I don't want to make any unfounded claims for the powers of mead, but I know that even the disbelievers will believe miracles if that bus full of old people comes back with a baby pram on the front.

About 80 percent of those old people could tell us a story about mead-making and mead drinking. One woman told me that she remembered when the children used to bring a bottle of mead to school to have with their lunch. That group kept coming back for over ten years, and of the new ones who joined the group, barely anyone could tell us about mead-making. In other words, mead-making in New Zealand was almost universal and then suddenly, over a ten-year period, it stopped.

It stopped because of electric lights. Once we got electric lights, people stopped making honey-mead. Anyone with a little intelligence can see why. Early on, people washed the beeswax to make candles, and the washings contained sweetness and was tossed into a barrel in the corner to ferment. If you wanted a nice, sweet, syrupy drink (remember they had no access to sugar), you could go to the barrel with your little cup, flick around in there, and have a nice drink. It was considered quite a nourishing drink. Then, once electricity came along, they didn't have to wash beeswax anymore, and mead-making virtually stopped and became a forgotten art in New Zealand.

The Christian churches were the biggest mead-makers in Europe for centuries. They were washing beeswax for the candles for the church ceremonies. Prior to the Reformation, one German church ordered 36,000 pounds of beeswax. We know from historical records that they had nineteen monks whose job it was to wash the wax, clean it, store the washings, ferment them, and then conduct what they called the "Church Ale." To our pagan ancestors, an "ale" was a party or celebration of great rejoicing. At the church "Ale," the fermented mead was sold to parishioners to make money to maintain the church buildings. The keystone above the door then read: "If it had not been for the ales, this church would never have been built." They were referring to the celebration, nothing to do with drink

But somewhere along the way, the word "ale" became corrupted with the demon booze. But the way I figure it, that became a problem for the good Father, and he had the "e" changed to "m." It then read that it was "alms" that built the church.

When the Reformation came to Europe, the pro-

After sampling some of Leon Havill's mead, this conference participant rests up for the Great American Beer Festival.

ceeds of the Church's mead-making went to fund the war, but the one country that wasn't touched by the Reformation was Poland. In Poland today, the products of nearly a million beehives go into mead each year. I believe it is either Poland's national drink, or at least one of its most popular drinks.

Traditionally the only the place you could get clear mead was if you were wealthy enough to store the mead for seven years. The only other place you could get mead was in Heaven. I just saw looks of disappointment cross several people's face. Well, look, just have an extra glass before you go in, case you lose out.

We call our company the Mazer Mead Company. The mazer was traditionally the cup or bowl from which the mead was drunk. Each person had a personal cup, and then there was a large communal bowl that was passed around. Often the family coat of arms was placed in the bottom of the cup, along with words of wisdom or warning. The mazer bowl was considered as part of the wealth of a man, and upon his death, it was always left to a son. The idea was that by encouraging the mead drinking, the male line of the family would continue. The word mazer actually came from the Olde English word *maeseren*, which was the name of maple wood. The cup or bowl was turned from the maple wood, and the little spots in the wood were known as the mazer, which we call "birdseye" maple.

I am told that the Germans had a similar cup. Everything about it was the same, with the same value, but they looked at the grain, and in the old Germanic language it was the *missel*. So the German cup became known as the missel cup.

The monks also had their cups, no where as valuable, of course, as the families' bowls. But they would carve their words of choice into the bottom of the bowl. The communal bowls were probably about eighteen inches across and four or five inches deep and held three bottles. After the monks had drunk the mead, they could gaze in upon the saint and thank the Lord for a wonderful, big taste of heaven. If someone drank too much from the cup, and got a little addled, he was said to be mazed. And in our language today, if someone has had too much to drink, he is said to be "mazy" in the head. If someone was walking, he was "afoot," if he was in bed, he was "abed," and if he had been to the cup, he was "amazed."

Many of you know that what the Vikings did to our Anglo-Saxon ancestors. They beat the hell out of them. But almost no one knows what our ancestors did to the Vikings. They gave them a pretty rough time, which are borne out by the rune stones in Scandanavia. It is recorded that a whole family of sons were drowned at sea or killed in various battles. The male population during this time in Scandinavia was being decimated. The Vikings were drinking tremendous quantities of mead during the long winter evenings. In the long halls at night, the cup would be passed around and everyone would drink. They even held drinking competitions, and most often the mead was drunk from the curved horns of the rams. A man would drink as much as he could from the horn and hand it to the judge for his opinion. How could he tell if the mead was around the corner of the horn? To overcome that problem in judging, the judge bored a series of holes down the sides of the horn and put in pegs. The judge then pulled the pegs out. The first one may have drunk down to peg five, the second to peg seven. So the second one, who pitted experience in drinking against youth, was said to have taken the first one down a peg or two.

One guy was able to drink the whole jolly lot in the horn. The judge removed all the pegs without finding a drop of mead inside. Then he proclaimed that the last drinker had "pegged out."

In another case, the warriors were going to battle, and they were wanting a quick drink of mead on the field. One man reached down and picked up the empty skull of a long-fallen enemy, and poured the mead into it. Then he passed the skull of mead to his companions. And from the time on, you could hear on the Scandinavian battlefields the men calling for a quick drink of mead: Skull! Skull! Or Skoal! Skoal!"

Another word that comes our way from mead is the honeymoon. At weddings, when the ceremony had been performed, the happy couple drank a considerable quantity of mead for one moon or month afterward. Then in nine months, if a son was born, the maker of the mead was commended. That has happened to us at our meadery. One woman in her mid-thirties came in and bought some mead, and in a few months she came back and grabbed my arm. She said, "You won't believe it. We've been married for years, never able to have any family. I took home three bottles of mead and since then have conceived twins."

I was very happy for her, of course. Then she added, "There was also a religious organization praying for us."

"Well, then," I said, "you must have got one from each."

I was telling a scientist one day about how mead was praised for causing sons to be born. He said, "Oh, that's old hat. We know all about that. If we breed three

Charlie Papazian, president of the American Homebrewers Association, dressed in his mead-drinking clothes, congratulates the 1988 Homebrew of the Year, John Maier, of Juneau, Alaska.

lines of female animals in a row, we know that at the end of three seasons we will have roughly fifty/fifty male and female off-spring. But if we alter the body pH of the females, over three seasons we can expect to get up to 80 percent male or 80 percent female depending on what we alter."

He went on to explain that under alkaline conditions in the female body, more males will be born. Under acid conditions, more females will be born. That must be why the Vikings encouraged mead-drinking.

About mead being an aphrodisiac, I know you are all skeptical. But remember that our ancestors were starved for sugar. Can you imagine a young couple with a wedding, the excitement, a new partner, being given vast quantities of sweet, syrupy mead? With that sudden increase in their blood sugar, they would have a lot of energy. They would wake in a veritable frenzy of lust!

We put corks in our mead in the interest of moderation. You can take the cork out, then recork it if you don't drink it all, and save it for later. The mead will still be good in quite a few months' time. We serve our mead at room temperature. Even you don't have a mazer cup, a coffee mug is good, especially if you have warmed it a little first. You take a sniff of the warm mead, and it imparts the fragrance of a cloverfield on a summer's day. When you have finished your fourth coffee mugful, just shut your eyes and listen. You can almost hear the pram wheels squeaking.

Sometimes we serve it as a long, cool drink with two parts mead, one part dry ginger ale and crushed mint leaves and slices of lemon for a summer cooler.

One lady in her sixties comes to the meadery and gets a dozen bottles every week. One day Gay said to me, "You say something to her about getting so much mead. She lives alone, after all."

The next time the lady came in, I was just about to open my mouth when she said, "I don't drink all of this by myself, of course. I'm a psychiatrist, and I recommend this to the people who come to me suffering from insomnia. I could prescribe drugs, but occasionally a person can get a drug problem. I just send them home with a bottle of mead. I tell them to take one small glass before they go to bed at night, and for 99 percent of them it works."

Now I know that one minute I am telling you mead is an aphrodisiac and the next minute I am saying that it puts you to sleep. Can you have both? The answer, of course, is yes. Don't be impatient. Wait for morning.

It doesn't work for everything, though, I must admit. One woman, who would be flattered if I said she was in her thirties came in. You know the type: she's no spring chicken, but she's still game. She had a glass or two of mead, and I told her, "One more glass of that, and you'll be anybody's."

"Oh, I got to that stage last night," she said, "and nobody wanted me."

I will close by reciting the motto of our meadery. Mead is said to make you invincible in war and irresistible in love. It also can improve your golf score. And so, to you I bid good health in the mazers of mead.

Leon Havill and his wife Gay make their honey mead called Havill's Mead in Rangiora, New Zealand.

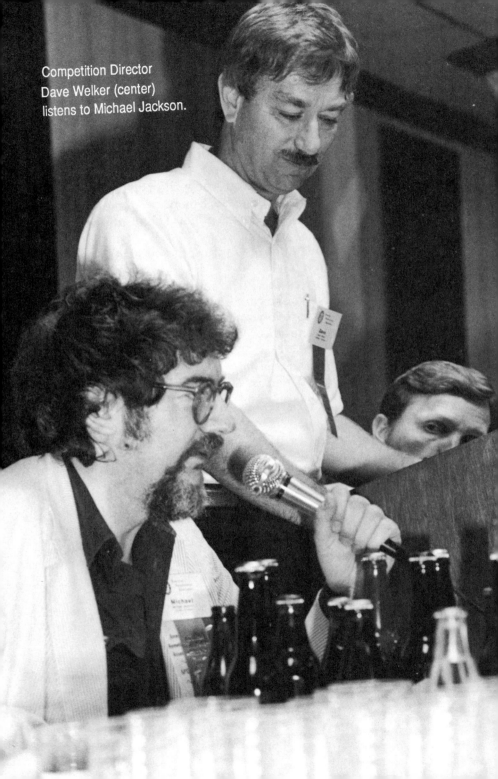

Competition Director
Dave Welker (center)
listens to Michael Jackson.

9.
Brewpubs in Austria

Baron Henrik Bachofen von Echt
Nussdorf's Brewery, Austria

I have never discovered how most people become beer brewers. Maybe they drink a beer, like it, and think they want to be involved in beer production Or maybe they drink a beer, don't like it, and believe there must be a better way to make beer. For me, it was easy to become involved in brewing as I was born into a brewing family, and am a sixth generation brewer. My dad gave me the advice: "Son, do something decent, don't become a beer brewer." You can see how successful he was in giving his advice.

I got my Ph.D in nuclear physics and chemistry and became a nuclear physicist. I joined Siemens, the German Electrical Company, and became project manager for Austria's first nuclear power plant. After I left Siemens, the whole thing became troublesome, and as you may know, that power plant never went into operation. And so, here I sit, a confirmed, old beer brewer.

To make a long story short, my family's brewery

was the Nussdorfer Brauerei founded in 1819. It had a maximum production of nearly 300,000 hectoliters. In 1950, it merged with Brauerei Schwechat and was dismantled. Then just like Oscar Wilde's "The Ghost Goes West," it was reconstructed in Agudos, Brazil, and in 1953, it began to produce Vienna Lager Beer. Today it is one of Brazil's biggest breweries.

In 1970, Brauerei Schwechat merged with Oester-reichische Brau AG, and together they became Austria's biggest brewing group with five breweries total and an output of 3.5 million hectoliters per year. While the management at Schwechat more or less did what I suggested, Dr. Christian Beurle, the general manager of Brau, listened very nicely to what I suggested and then did precisely what he wanted. I have to admit, however, that he was right in some cases. Now my package of shares in Brau AG is small enough where I no longer have the influence to tell him what to do.

In 1983, two things happened. The pubbrewery technology that had started in the United Kingdom had developed to the point where a person could start a small brewery with a relatively small investment. The second was that the 30,000-square-foot cellars in my private castle became partly vacant. This caused me to begin thinking seriously about starting a small, new brewery in Nussdorf.

To begin, I contacted eight companies that were able to offer brewery equipment. One of them, NERB/ Freysing in Bavaria, didn't even bother to answer my inquiries. Another one, Steincker, gave a fancy offer, but it was far too expensive. A third offered used equipment that was too small. Brewland, a British equipment furnisher, was a little too primitive. Schultz/Bamberg, which I liked the most, seemed a little too expensive since at that time I didn't know whether the project would be profitable. BAM (Bayerische Aluminium Werke) and Dipl.Ing Rudolf Caspary had very nice designs but had not yet built a brewery. Finally, SPR, a British company in Manchester, offered equipment that was nice and was within my budget. Also, Mr. Ward of SPR had a great deal of experience in brewing British beers.

What we tried to do, when we gave the order for the brewery, was to pack Central European technology into SPR's British construction. The result was probably perfect for brewing an excellent Lancastrian Ale, but that was about it. And our Central European customers are used to a little different type of taste. It took us about half a year of adding equipment, welding pipes into the system, and putting in valves before we arrived at a point where we were satisfied with the quality of the beer and our customers were also happy. Now we are able to produce every type of beer our customers could possible ask for.

When it was complete, our plant finally consisted of a two-roller malt mill; a grist case with an auger to bring the grist to the mash and lauter tun; and a mash and lauter tun with an integrated premasher, a lauterscreen and a rake with twelve turns per minute. We had a gas-fired copper kettle with an impeller; a whirlpool; a hot-water tank with a 10 kilowatt heating element; a paraflow; two individually cooled fermenters; and one caustic and one acid CIP tank. There were ten conditioning tanks that were placed in a cold room, a sterile air compressor, two chamber-sheet filters, two pressure tanks, a complete automatic keg-washer, and a used

Richard Gleeson (left) and Michael Jackson, two judges in the final round of the National Homebrew Competition, discuss the qualities of their category.

rebuilt bottle-filler, crown corker, and labeller. Also there were many pumps, hoses, a packer, and many, many tools. You can't imagine how many tools we have bought during the last three years. We could probably build a jet airplane with them.

The equipment was planned to produce ten Imperial barrels, which is equal to 16.4 hectoliters. However, we asked the manufacturer to build the equipment a little bit bigger for expansion. Today our brew length is twenty hectoliters, which works perfectly for us.

In the meantime, we also made a primitive bottle-washer, which has brushes. In Austria, we use returnable bottles. We get them from the glass factory absolutely sterile, bottle without washing them, and then see only about 20 percent of these bottles come back to us again. We bring those that are returned to us to a soft-drink producer next door,who washes them for us.

The total investment for the brewing equipment, including bringing the building into shape, was close to $450,000 U.S. That was four years ago.

Once the equipment was in place, we were able to produce beer. If we were to serve only at home to family and guests, one brew would have lasted for almost a year. So we were obliged to sell most of our production. I have to admit that I would never have thought of starting a pubbrewery had I not had a contract in my pocket to sell the beer.

When we initiated the brewery, it was our general idea that it would take us about two years to get our technology into operation. During that time, we wouldn't have time to go out and sell the beer, so someone else would have to do that job. Then an idea was born. Since we had a lot of friends in the brewing business, we would offer our beer specialties to them that they could not brew on a profitable basis in order to round out their production line. This worked, but not perfectly.

I went to Dr. Beurle and asked him to sell our beer through his channels. He was very scared, however, that there would be a huge discussion about the difference between commercially made beer and handmade beer. I called my friends at Anheuser-Busch in St. Louis and asked them what was being done in the United States. They told me that in the United States there was a microbrewery going up every second week, and another one closing down every month.

"The quantities they produce are negligible," my friends said. "But if people talk about those microbrewer-

Conference participants learn to recognize different flavors and aromas in doctored beer.

ies and their beer, it is good for every beer producer."

That straightened out my attitude, and I went to Austria's second biggest brewing group, Steirerbrau. The general manager there, Dr. Weitzendorff, thought I had a great idea and offered to take my beer immediately into his production line. However, I had a little suspicion that his enthusiam for my beer wasn't as great as his motivation to do something mean to his bigger competitor on the Austrian market. As soon as the news got to the journalists, the newspapers and the radio and television stations were full of the story that one of Brau AG's major shareholders had built a small brewery and that Brau AGs biggest competitor was handling its distribution.

At that time, our plan was to offer our beer only in kegs and sell it to other breweries. Our customers would then have access to our product in pubs and restaurants. We couldn't have had better advertising. But at the time this was on television, our beer wasn't available in every pub. The customers who were trying to get our beers couldn't always find it, and after a while, they forgot about it. As the saying goes: "There is nothing older then yesterday's newspaper."

In the long-term, this strategy was absolutely wrong, even though we had no financial problems and our production went smoothly with Steirerbrau. The problem was that you can't train and motivate salespeople in a big brewery, who one day speak in terms of truckloads of beer and big discounts, to go out and sell small quantities of beer at high prices.

So we had to change our strategy. Although we only wanted to keg our beer originally, we had to start bottling. We began using a Champagne filler, and today we use an old filler that handles 3,500 bottles per hour.

When we started to brew beer, our only product was a stout, Sir Henry's Stout. Half a year later, we began experimenting with a recipe that my grandfather's dad had used last century. From it, we produced Nussdorfer St. Thomasbrau, a Bavarian type alt-beer. The market was asking for light, bright beer, so we also created the double-hopped Nussdorfer Doppelhopfen Hell. It is somewhat similar to a Kolsch-type beer. Our last creation was adding 15 percent whisky malt to the malt used in St. Thomas. In doing so, Nussdorfer Old Whisky Beer was born. The whisky malt comes from France, and you would be interested to know that two-thirds of Scottish whisky is produced with fresh malt.

All our beers are top-fermented. And while every-

Mark Carpenter (center), Anchor Brewing Company, accepts a Gold Medal for his Anchor Porter, from Charlie Papazian (left) and Daniel Bradford.

one else does a six-pack; we do a seven-pack. These stack on a pallet wonderfully, and you almost don't have to shrink the pallet to stabilize it.

As Austria's smallest little brewery, as we call ourselves, we are now producing four varieties of beer, and my brewmaster, Dipl. Ing. Otto Schmied, thinks that his boss has gone completely crazy. But as today's situation shows, this production strategy was absolutely successful.

Generally speaking, I have to admit that within the last three-and-a-half years, there did exist moments when I doubted whether I was doing the right thing. I am very grateful to Michael Jackson who straightened my backbone and told me that I was on the right track and should take it more seriously than I do. In his Pocket Guide to Beer (1986), he decorated our Sir Henry's Stout with three stars, which was the best he had to give for an Austrian beer. That made me very proud.

As a byproduct to Nussdorf's beer production, people have asked if we would plan and furnish small breweries. We are doing so. We have specialized in small breweries fully equipped with kegging and bottling. We start at 1,000 hectoliters per year and offer microbreweries with a maximum capacity of 25,000 hectoliters. For very, very small pubbreweries, we refer people to our competitors, particularly to his Royal Highness Prince Luitpold.

In 1986, we sold a plant to owners in Hawaii, which is in operation at this time. This year (1988), one of our plants in Nigeria should go into operation. Next year we believe that our client in Albuquerque, New Mexico, will be producing beer.

When we started bottling our beer at Brauhaus Nussdorf, we priced it at twice the price of a normal beer in Austria. Sales trickled in. After a time, we tripled our price, and sales went up a little. Then we asked four times the price of a standard beer, and now we can't produce as much beer as our customers would like to have.

One of the reasons for our success is definitely our brewpub. In 1986, we opened a little restaurant with approximately eighty places to sit at tables and a couple of old wooden barrels as stand-up bars. This year, we also opened a little beergarden. Besides the beer, we serve very spicy foods like soups, sausages, and sandwiches.

In the beginning we were open Friday to Monday, from noon to evening. After some experimentation, we decided that we had to stay open seven days a week. The earnings at lunchtime were not large enough, however, so we decided to open at 4 p.m. We sell food until 10 p.m. and beer until midnight.

When we first opened, we were crowded, but then came days when there were few customers. In 1987, we had an average of 140 customers per day. This year, once we opened the beer garden with its fifty additional seats, we have 200 customers a day. I called home yesterday, and we were already booked up for Friday, Saturday, and Sunday.

Last year, we sold 2,096 hectoliters of beer. One-third was sold at the pub in glasses and mugs, one-third was carried away in our seven-pack or party kegs, and one-third went to supermarkets. This year, we expect to sell 3,000 to 3,500 hectoliters: one-sixth at the pub, one-sixth take-home, and two-thirds through supermarkets.

All I can tell you is that when I started, I had a lot of doubts. Now I am happy with the project, and it is wonderful.

Baron Bachofen is the founder of a brewpub overlooking Nussdorf's Brewery. In 1983, he planned his microbrewery. In 1984, he produced his first test brew. In 1987, his establishment attracted 50,000 guests.

Ed Stoudt (left), Stoudt Brewing Company,
sets up his table at the Festival.

10.
Beer for Lunch

Michael Jackson
Author and Bard of Beer

In the presentations by Prince Luitpold and Baron Bachofen von Echt, we heard about Germany and Austria, two countries in which beer is often served with food. Indeed, in Czechoslovakia, Austria, and Germany, beer is generally taken as the normal beverage with food, and wine is often presented as an after-dinner drink, much as a liqueur would be. Until recently, beer in those countries was presented with very typical beer foods—sausages and legs of pork. In fact, nearly everything you eat in Germany turns out to be a leg of pork. I wonder what happens to the rest of the pig? I suppose there are lots of pigs in wheel chairs.

But those traditional menus are changing, especially in the brewpubs in Germany. A lot of the brewpubs are serving what I would call cuisine bourgeoise, a slightly more adventurous style of menu. Often also, chefs do little tricks like making the bread out of the spent grain from

the brewery.

In Britain we tend to regard beer as a drink to relax over when you are talking with your friends. In America it tends to be regarded as something you reward yourself with after you work hard. You mow the lawn and then you have a beer; and then maybe you watch a ball game and you have a beer. That is the underlying theme of most American beer advertising, which makes it very difficult for people who are homebrewers and who love beer and then go into commercial brewing making specialty beers. Those beers are not lawn-mowing beers, and yet all the consumer knows about is lawn-mowing beers. You make a great beer and the consumer finds it thick, heavy, bitter, and unpleasant like cough medicine. It is not the consumer's fault; he has never experienced a different kind of beer, in a different context—as an aperitif, as a wonderful digestive, as a splendid nightcap.

I like to show different beers in as many different contexts as I possibly can, and that is how Charlie Papazian came to ask me to host lunches like this one. This one is my third, and these are not haute cuisine meals. They are cuisine bourgeoise. I cannot take credit for the food, as that is the chef's domain, but these are my ideas of how beer can be used in food—a sauce made from raspberry beer and on the pate a slightly marmaladey sauce with Belgian framboise. But let us begin our meal with a Duvel.

I would like to tell you a bit about both the beer that is used in our food and also the beer that I recommend that we drink with it. I mentioned we used raspberry beer. It is a Lambic, which is a type of wheat beer made with wild yeast as a wine traditionally was. The name Lambic originates from the town of Lembeek in Belgium, just to the west of Brussels. There are about ten very small breweries in the area that make Lambic beer. A Lambic has an original gravity of 12 to 13 degrees Plato, and is made with 30 to 40 percent unmalted wheat with the remainder a malted barley. Because of that very high proportion of unmalted wheat, it has a milky-white wort that has to be boiled for a very long time—about three to six hours. The hops that are used are aged so they won't be aromatic. That is exactly the opposite of the normal procedure. Instead of wanting fresh hops, which most brewers do, Lambic brewers want aged hops because they don't want flavor and aroma from the hops. What they want is the antiseptic value of the hops; in other words, the very original use of the hop.

The wort is exposed to the atmosphere in an open cooler in the eaves of the roof of the brewhouse, where it is infected by the wild yeasts of the area. It is then put into unlined wooden casks that have been previously used for making claret, port, sometimes even sherry. The casks contain their own microflora, so the fermentation is a combination of the wild yeast in the atmosphere and the wild microflora that exists in the brewery, which is intentionally not kept particularly clean. The principal bacteria involved are *Brettanomyces Lambicus* named after the town.

Primary fermentation takes about six days, but the secondary can go on from three months to a year. At that stage the beer is called young beer. It is then blended with beer that has been kept for three years, and a new fermentation starts. Then if it is a raspberry beer, raspberries are added when they are picked at harvest time and are left in the beer until September or October. During that time, the sugar in the raspberries ferments and produces not a huge sweet fruitiness, but a dry fruitiness with a great deal of aroma.

Some of the breweries use fresh fruit; some make a syrup of fresh fruits; some use extracts. I think if they use extracts, which is really cheating, they produce a very bonbon, candyish taste. If anybody has the opportunity to go to Belgium and would like to taste a very true, whole fruit Belgian framboise, he or she should stop in at the Canpillon brewery in Brussels, which makes a wonderful framboise.

The beer we are drinking with this sauce is Duvel, also a Belgian beer. I thought it would make a nice accompaniment because it is quite a fruity tasting beer. Of course it is not a beer with fruit in it. In a way, it is a diametrical opposite, from a production viewpoint, to the Lambic beer. A Lambic type is the most primitive type of beer commercially produced and marketed as a beer, whereas Duvel is really a highly sophisticated product made in a very modern block brewhouse that looks a bit like a laundromat.

Duvel is an all-malt beer made with two-row malt—mainly from Denmark. The brewery does its own malting to a very pale specification. The EBC on the beer is about 6.5. Its original gravity is 17.5 degrees Plato, or about 1070. It doesn't taste to me like a strong beer, but it is deceptively strong. The word Duvel means devil, a very good name for it.

One interesting fact about Duvel is that Jean de Clerck, the famous Belgian brewing scientist, obtained some McEwan's yeast from Scotland as its basis. He found twenty different strains in the yeast and isolated single cells from them. Then, in the 1930s, he used one of those cells to brew Duvel.

Duvel is a top-fermenting beer. It is cold conditioned at 32 degrees F for two or three weeks, bottled with the yeast in the bottle, then warm-conditioned for one to two weeks before it is given another cold conditioning at 38 degrees F for a month or more. It is a hoppy beer with 31 units of bitterness, but very much Saaz hop character. It is one of the few top-fermenting beers that is very good served extremely cold. It reminds me a little bit of those neutral-colored brandies from Alsace that are known as white alcohols.

In the first course of this meal, I am trying to achieve a combination of fruity notes—a fruity source and a fruity beer to go with it. I suggested to Vince, the chef, that the main course emphasize certain aromatic characters. So we have lamb cooked in juniper berries. Juniper berries are quite a traditional flavoring in food, and especially in lamb. They also are used to aromatize beer. Just as the Belgians have used fruits, so have berries, tree barks, and all sorts of other substances been used as an aromatizing ingredient.

Once I ran across a juniper berry beer made in the United States, although that brewery no longer exists. There is a juniper beer made in Belgium and one made in Sweden. We don't have a juniper beer to use in the cooking here, but to complement the aromatic, slightly phenolic quality of junipers ,we have used a smoked beer, a Rauchbier from Bamberg in the northern part of Bavaria. Two breweries there produce Rauchbier, one a very tiny house brewery called Zymspezial, and the other a slightly larger one called Schlenkerla. The beer we have used in the cooking today is made in Eltmann, a small town adjoining Bamberg. Rauchbier is traditionally made from malt that has been smoked over beechwood.

I wanted us to have an aromatic beer to drink with this dish. Lamb is something we eat a lot of in England, especially in the southeast of the country. So I selected a very aromatic beer from that area of England, Young's Special London Ale. The local pub near my home in London is owned by the Young's brewery. It has two regular bitters on draft. One is a very bitter, very low-gravity beer that is packed with taste. There also is a special bitter, a 1.046, the bottled counterpart of which is called Ramrod. Then there is the Special London Ale, a sort of super premium bitter. It has an original gravity of 1.062, alcohol of 4.8 to 5percent by weight, and 50 Bitterness Units. To my taste, it has a hop garden in every bottle.

What we are going to have next is a very American apple pie—a pie cooked with Thomas Hardy ale. Thomas Hardy ale is produced by the Eldridge Pope brewery in the west of England. Pope is a very nice, old-fashioned brewery, very traditionalist, and very quality-oriented. It brews a full range of ales that all have a rather soft, fruity character to them from the house yeasts. The brewhouse is a traditional copper brewhouse. The open fermenters are of the design you may have seen sometimes in Britain; they look a little bit like railway wagons from the outside. Pope very heavily uses Fuggles and Goldings hops in its beers.

This particular product is made entirely with pale ale malt, which I guess it is the British counterpart of Vienna malts. The malt is made entirely from the British variety Maris Otter, which is regarded by many British ale brewers as being the best variety from which to make ale malts. The beer starts from a gravity of 1125.8, so it is nudging 30 degrees Plato. At that gravity, even a pale ale malt produces a pretty full color. The beer is dry hopped. The yeast is pitched twice in fermentation and a third time in the conditioning period. The beer has three months of conditioning in a tank, and it is then bottled with a very high level of residual sugar and yeast in it. It should be at least five years old before it is served. People may think it is rather snobbish for beer, not only wine, to have vintage dates, but if you drink this beer in under five years, it is excessively syrupy.

This is a beer that was first brewed in 1968 to mark the fortieth anniversary of the death of the poet and novelist Thomas Hardy. There was a literary festival to celebrate Hardy's work in Dorchester—where Hardy lived and worked and where the brewery is. Thomas Hardy wrote quite a lot about Pope and the beer in Dorchester, so the brewery returned the compliment by naming one of its beers after him, albeit after his death.

I recently performed a tasting of all of the vintages of Thomas Hardy from 1968 to the present. The very early ales have a very Madeira-like quality that I thought would go very well in an apple pie. Vinney and I also wanted to have a cream or custard or ice cream to go with it.

The beer to be enjoyed with this wonderful dessert is Celebrator, a double Bock beer from the Ayinger Brewery in Germany. In Germany it is known as "Fortunator." Its gravity is about 18 to 18.5, or 1.072 to 1.074, with about 6 percent alcohol by weight. It has three different malts and about three months of aging. It is a sweet, smooth, rich beer that I thought would be a nice dessert beer today.

I suggested we use Anchor Wheat beer in the creme Anglaise because most wheat beers have a little tinge of apples, or a plummy or honey sweet note that would go very well with a cream made for a fruit pie. The wheat beers made in Berlin use a symbiosis of lactobacillus and yeast called *Lactobacillus delbruckii*. Dr. Max Delbruck first isolated the particular bacillus at the University of Berlin Brewing Institute. In the south of Germany, wheat beers generally use a top-fermenting yeast. This style of yeast releases certain phenols during fermentation that produce a clovelike character that is very nice with sweet things like apple pies.

American wheat beers, of which there are about twenty, have covered the waterfront of different tastes. No one has tried to work with lactobacillus in a controlled way in America. But if Mark Carpenter from Anchor is here, I believe he should be the one to tell you about his wheat beer.

Mark Carpenter
We started making wheat beer in 1984. Until that time all of our beers had been in the English style, with the exception of our Steam beer. Foghorn was our first very unusual brew, followed by our porter, our ales, and our Christmas ales. We decided it would be a challenge to make a light beer, but we didn't want to make a light lager beer that would be in competition with the large American breweries. So we looked around the world at the styles of brewing that weren't light in character, and we saw wheat beers.

At first, we tried many wheat beers and went to

The Bard of Beer,
Michael Jackson,
in his studio.

Germany to see wheat beers being made. We liked many of them, but we didn't think that the Bavarian yeast flavor, the "wild yeast" flavor, was something we wanted in ours. We wanted something to our taste, to the American taste, that was a little cleaner flavor in the palate.

We decided to use a pure top-fermenting ale yeast, and as much wheat as we possibly could. As you may know, run-off is a problem in the lauter tun when you use too much wheat; you need the husk from the barley to aid in filtering the mash. We started out at about 60 percent wheat in our first wheat beers and tried a few tricks. We put spent hops in with the mash to aid in filtering because we had heard a few German brewmasters tried that. We tried mashing temperatures that started at 98 degrees F and stopped at about seven different places on the way up to about 160 degrees. We started out with Saaz hops because we really liked their flavoring character. The original gravity of our wheat beer is about 11.

From time to time, we have changed our wheat beer. We don't have it in a six-pack yet because the changes are still being made. Someday, when we decide on what we really like, we probably will come out with a six-pack and cases.

This particular wheat beer is about 73 percent malted wheat, and it is entirely hopped with a single addition at the start of the boil with Kent Goldings that we have carefully aged for a year to have a better dry hopping value, although we don't use them for that reason. We like Kent Goldings very much, and if there is anything I would criticize about them it is that they are a little too light. But they produce a very light, clean, nice wheat beer. And I think it is certainly a wonderful dessert.

Michael Jackson

If you have been behaving yourself and waited for the last beer, you may now open our after-dinner drink, Sierra Nevada Big Foot Barley Wine. This is the strongest beer in America and is intended to be treated as a digestive, a Cognac.

Big Foot has an original gravity of 1.095 and is just under 8.5 percent alcohol by weight. I find it a hugely tasty, complex, and very strong-tasting beer. I thought it would be a nice beer to finish off our lunch.

I really enjoyed the beers that we have had here today, both in the cooking and also to drink. I believe this is an area that has a great deal of potential in the future.

Michael Jackson, Bard of Beer, is known worldwide for his love of all things good, and especially good beer. He is the author of the Simon and Schuster Pocket Guide to Beer *and the newly revised* New World Guide to Beer. *He is a contributor to* zymurgy, The New Brewer, Playboy, *and* The Washington Post, *among many other newspapers and magazines.*

A happy GABF beer-lover.

11.
Hop Flavor in Beer

George Fix ,Ph.D.
Professor of Science

When I reflect on brewing science, it strikes me
how specialized it is and how important are the roles of
beer constituents. As brewers, the issues we face are very
special, and brewing science has developed as a subject
with its own unique features. From the beginning, brewing science has been a user science. For example, Louis
Pasteur, who was one of the first to make progress in this
area, got started with a grant from the French govern-
ment. He had a very well-defined goal: to find out why
French beer was so wretched. That set the tone for the
future of the subject.

As a user science, brewing science has two basic
objectives: to clarify and to simplify the description of processes that are fundamental to brewing. The ideal is to
provide a broad base of knowledge that on one hand is
accessible to brewers and on the other hand is technically
accurate and relevant, meaning that it addresses real,
basic issues as opposed to esoteric sidelines. Generally

Dr. George Fix

this type of progress takes time. For example, when evidence first appeared showing that the mash has proteins and enzymes that are responsible for starch conversion and related activities, brewers were fairly skeptical. Now, thanks to the clarification of these issues, we use this knowledge daily in our brewing.

Unfortunately, not all areas have progressed as far as others. For example, when the unsuspecting brewer turns to the literature for guidance and insight on how beer takes on hop characteristics, he is typically greeted with complicated reaction systems that even those with a good background in chemistry would regard as esoteric. The conclusion reached is another source of frustration. For example, a famous paper on hops, where in excess of thirty different reaction systems were developed, concluded with the following statement, "Hop chemistry is complicated and still poorly understood. Thus the best we can say is that some of these reaction mechanisms may be relevant. On the other hand, none of them may be relevant."

At this point there may be some people in the audience wondering why one would want to give a lecture on hops given these complications. Thus a few brief words of explanation are perhaps in order.

Several years ago I started the project of trying to write a book on brewing science that was user-oriented. It is not meant to be a chemistry or biology book, but is meant to deal with some of the basic issues that for example were raised in Jean de Clerck's classic two-volume monograph. (This is now out of print.) At the start, I deliberately ignored all the material on hops until the very end, probably hoping that it would go away. After completing the other parts of the book in mid-1987, I sat down and went through my folder on hops, which contained articles, data, and a list of experiments I wanted to do. I discovered something important in the process; namely, that in a perfect world, populated by perfect people, a complete understanding of everything would be the only real objective. However, in an imperfect world, populated by imperfect people (I must acknowledge a life-long membership in that group), a reasonable alternative is to develop a very clear understanding of what we do know and what we do not know. Preparing the material for my book along those lines resolved a lot of misconceptions. In the end, I would regard the experience as one of practical value as far as my personal brewing is concerned, and I hope a few others of you might find the same.

My subject matter falls into two parts: Everything You Ever Wanted to Know About Bitterness Units and Going Beyond Bitterness Units. The second part is motivated by the experience of having two beers in front of me that were very similar in style, brewing materials, and Bitterness Units. Yet these two beers had an overall hop flavor (which means both taste and smell) that was different. I believe that the examples of this are so common that we have to admit that Bitterness Units in and of itself is an imperfect measure of hop flavor.

This shouldn't surprise us. There is not a person in this room who couldn't think of brews that have been rescued from mediocrity or blandness by a pleasing, intriguing, well-developed hop profile. In terms of traditional beer styles, hops, along with ethanol, are the two major products in the sense that they occur in at least two times their flavor threshold. Because of the diversity and

Dr. George Fix

Table 1
Storage History

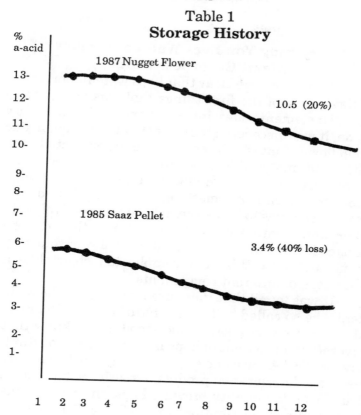

importance of hops, it is too much to expect that one single number could characterize their effect, be it Bitterness Units or some other measure. And so I will explore in the second part of my talk some of those things that are not measured by Bitterness Units in an attempt to reach some practical criteria we can use in designing the overall hop character of our beers.

Everything You Ever Wanted to Know
About Bitterness Units

When it became clear that hops were important to beer flavor, one of the first things that was done was to break their elements down into smaller constituents. Very early on, it was discovered that it is the sticky resin inside the hop flower that is of interest. It can be extracted from the hop and analyzed. One strategy that has been well used in brewing is the "divide and conquer" strategy. Rather than tackling something very complicated like resins, the secret is to break them down progressively into simpler units until we obtain something that can be understood. Once we are at that stage, we work our way back up and view this very complicated object like a kaleidoscope of different components.

It was found that there are two parts to the resin content: the so-called "soft" and "hard" resins. Whereas, hard resins are very poorly understood, we do know that the overall resin content of hops is more or less constant. Soft resins do decrease and so presumably hard resins are some sort of deterioration product. Experience has shown that in fresh, top-quality brewing hops, the hard resins make only minor contributions to hop flavor. Thus from a practical point of view, we can confine our attention to the soft resins (although for old hops this assumption could be questioned).

The soft resins can be broken down into three smaller fractions: the beta acids, the alpha acids, and uncharacterized soft resins. The uncharacterized soft resins are not understood at all. Like the hard resins, experience has shown that with top-quality brewing hops in good condition, we can ignore this faction with a reason-

Dr. George Fix points out the vital significance of hop flavor characters.

able degree of confidence. But as the hop ages, again this assumption become shakier.

Some progress has been made in understanding the role of beta acids in recent years. They do add a bitter to beer, but with fresh hops this is generally secondary to the mellow and pleasing bitter from the alpha acids. Experimental brews made with beta acid extracts have shown that beta acids contribute "hop cling" (aftertaste) and are somewhat harsh although mild in taste and smell.

An important point to be made about alpha acids is that they deteriorate early via oxidation during storage. By reducing the storage temperature, the oxidation rates can be lowered, but even at 32 degrees F it is important to limit exposure to air. Another factor to keep in mind is that there is a large difference in hop varieties with respect to stability in storage. In addition, for any given variety, pellets will generally store better than flowers because of the more favorable surface area to volume ratios found in the former.

To illustrate these effects I will present storage data using two hops, namely 1987 Nugget flowers and 1985 Saaz pellets. The former is a new "high alpha" variety developed as a replacement for older high alpha hops like Bullion and Brewers Gold, both of which have very poor storage stability. Saaz is a world-class aroma hop that also has poor storage stability. The hops were obtained from a commercial brewery very shortly after being released, and they were stored in food bags at 32 degrees F. Alpha acid measurements were made on a monthly basis, and the data are shown in Table 1.

Observe that the Nugget lives up to its reputation as being stable in storage; however, even in this case there was a 20 percent loss of alpha acids after twelve months. The alpha acid loss on the Saaz hops was far more serious, as expected. The careful brewer would want to take these losses into account in the determination of hop usage rates.

Dr. George Fix

The other factor to take into account is the extent to which alpha acids are converted (isomerized) in the kettle boil. Alpa acids are not particularly soluble in wort; however, under boiling conditions their structure is "tweaked," giving rise to the more soluble iso-alpha acids. There is no part of brewing that is less understood than this one, and as a consequence brewers have introduced a "fudge factor" called the kettle utilization rate to deal with this situation. The latter is defined as follows:

Kettle Utilization = $\dfrac{\text{iso-alpha acids dissolved in wort (mg/l)}}{\text{alpha acids added (mg/l).}}$

While this "ignorance factor" covers up a lot of poorly understood processes, it tends to be fairly robust and varies only with a small number of things. The most important are the following:

(1) Time and temperature of the boil after hops were added.

(2) Wort gravity is a very important effect, and there is a fairly sharp decline in utilization as the wort gravity increases (especially over 13 to 14 degrees P).

(3) Kettle utilization does not vary significantly with hop variety, but utilization tends to be higher for pellets than hop leaves. It is not uncommon for the former to yield rates in the range .28 to .34 (28 to 34 percent), while yields with hop flowers typically come out near .20 to .28 (20 to 28 percent).

(4) A very important effect that is often overlooked is the role played by the pH of the wort being boiled. Kettle utilization does increase with pH, but so does the extraction of undesirable hop constituents. After several brew-

ing experiments this year I have come to the definite opinion that the best hop bitter (be it at a lower kettle utilization) is achieved by keeping the wort pH below 5.5 and preferably below 5.3. This effect is sufficiently significant in that water treatment should be employed if necessary to obtain this goal.

To illustrate these ideas, consider a sample brew where our target is to achieve a specific Bitterness Unit of 30 mg/l. This means there will be approximately 30 mg/l of iso-alpha acids dissolved in the beer. Suppose we consider two cases, one using six-month-old Nugget flowers, and another using six-month-old Saaz pellets. From Table 1 we see the Nuggets have an alpha acid of 12.2 percent, while the Saaz have an alpha acid of 4.2 percent. In addition, suppose we have a kettle utilization of 26 percent for the flowers and 31 percent for the pellets. At this point we have all the information we need to complete the correct amount of hops to be added. The calculations shown here are a mere exercise in common sense.

Sample Brew

Target: 30 mg/l   iso-a-acids

Nugget Flowers:

$$\text{Kettle utilization} = 26\%$$

$$a\text{ - acids required} = \frac{30}{.26} = 115.4 \text{ mg/l}$$

$$a\text{ - acid of hop} = 12.2\%$$

$$\text{Hops required} = \frac{115.4}{.122} = 945.8 \text{ mg/l} = .95 \text{ g/l}$$

(approximately 1/8 oz. per gallon)

Dr. George Fix

Saaz Pellets:

Kettle utilization $= 31\%$

a - acids required $= \dfrac{30}{.31}$ $= 96.8$ mg/l

a - acid of hop $\quad = 4.2\%$

Hops required $\quad = \dfrac{96.8}{.042} = 2304.1$ mg/l $= 2.3$ g/l

(approximately 1/3 oz. per gallon)

Two final effects relating to Bitterness Units should be cited. Because of their aromatic ring structure both alpha acids and iso-alpha acids readily oxidize, and the effects on the hop flavor of the finished beer can be significant. Excessive air pickup should be avoided, and this is as important during hot wort production as it is during the final stages of the fermentation and aging. An example of the ill effects of oxidation is when you have a fresh, new beer with a beautiful hop glow, and then some time later, perhaps a month or so, the hop aroma is gone. There may be some beta, some bitter, some cling, but the mellow glow is gone. All in all, the stability of your hop flavoring is one of the best ways of assessing how well you are doing in excluding oxidation.

Another effect that should not be overlooked is the masking effect of carbon dioxide (CO_2) on hop flavoring. An increase in CO_2 volumes from the normal range, 2.3 to 2.5 to 2.8 to 3.0, can readily be determined in otherwise identical beers in blind triangular tasting. As brewers, we can control our CO_2 volumes with some precision, and the

Table 2
Gas Chromatogram of Beer Flavor Compounds
and Hop-Derived Sesquiterpenoids

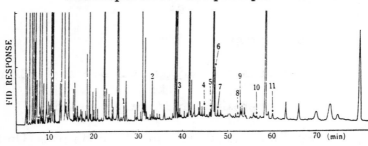

1, *Linalool*
2, *Alpha-Terpineol*
3, *Geraniol*
4, *Caryophyllene epoxide*
5, *Humulene epoxide I*
6, *Humulene epoxide II*

7, *Nerolidol*
8, *Humulol*
9, *T-Cadinol*
10, *Compound of peak No. 44*
11, *Humulenol II*

effort taken to do this will yield beer with better hop flavoring.

Going Beyond Bitterness Units

If you look at the older references, they focus entirely on the Humulone and Myrcene oils. Humulone is said to be important because the older Nobel hops, Saaz for example, are dominated by this characteristic oil. If you have ever smelled Saaz in the kettle, you will probably have noted an elegant, refined, and beautiful aroma. On the other hand, the Northern Brewer is dominated by Myrcene. Its flavoring tends to be a little more pungent.

This categorization is unsatisfying, however, because these two oils don't really describe some important and interesting hops. For example, Cascade has a very distinct and unique floral characteristic that is all its own. And it has nothing to do with those two hop oils. What gives Cascade this flavor? Dr. Peacock at Oregon State has done excellent work in this area with a technique called *gas chromatography*. The separation techniques used for alpha acids do not work for hop oils. Hop oils are too light and delicate. The key to the success of gas chromatography is it first transforms the hop oils into the gaseous state and separates them in this phase. This permits very accurate measurement.

A gas chromatograph of a typical hop oil registers both very large and very tiny peaks. An example is shown in Table 2. Some of the largest peaks show constituents in the parts per thousands. Remarkably, these are of absolutely no relevance whatsoever to beer flavor. They are very high in concentration, but they are flavorless. However, those with much less concentration give hop flavoring its primary aspects. Those measured in parts per billion are the most important for beer taste.

Because of these effects, it is necessary to adjoin "sniffers" to the chromatograph in order to ascertain which elements are of sensory significance.

Dr. Peacock took the gas chromatograph with the sniffer and did a thorough analysis on Cascade hops in attempting to discover what factors are crucial in distinguishing Cascade from other hops. She found that two alcohols, namely Germanoil and Linalool, are primarily responsible for the floral character of Cascades. In addition, she suggested use of a Floral Index, which measures the concentration of these hop oil constituents, as a guide to Cascade usage in practical brewing. The value of this

Table 3
Wye Target Hop Oil: Simultaneous
Flame Ionization and Sniffer Detection

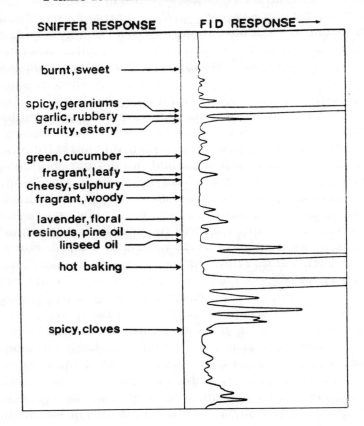

concept, particularly in post-fermentation hopping, is likely to be quite important.

The chromatograph has become a useful tool for

Dr. George Fix

brewers in other areas. For example, a couple of years ago, the English hop farmers oversulfured their crops because of various climatic conditions. Even after the drying period, sulfur constitutents still remained in many English hops. They made their way into the cask, and the brewers began screaming, not knowing what had happened to the flavors of their dry hopped ales. The Brewing Research Institute ran a chromatograph of various hop samples and readily identified a variety of sulfury constituents ranging from spicy and garlicy to cheesy and rubbery. An example chromatograph is shown in Table 3. Once this analysis was complete, the reasons for the defective flavors became apparent.

Another example comes from Japan. I was in that country a few years ago and took the opportunity to visit a few of their breweries. At the time, they were having some problems with their domestic hops. Because of agricultural import restrictions, foreign hops are limited and quite expensive for Japanese brewers. On the other hand, the most important of their domestic hops had a strong "herbal" character, which they wanted to keep under control in their beers.

To tackle this problem, they launched a chromatographic analysis with the goal of identifying the "herbal constituent," quantifying it, and using this index as a guide to how much of the domestic hops would be used. A preliminary analysis yielded a variety of oxidized flavors ranging from sagebrush to haylike but no herbal constituent. Finally a more detailed analysis yielded a tiny peak (marked No. 11 in Table 4) that is the herbal character. Its structure is unknown, and its concentration is in fractions of parts per trillion. Yet it is the controlling element in the

Table 4
Herbal Hop Oil Fraction: Simultaneous
Flame Ionization and Sniffer Detection

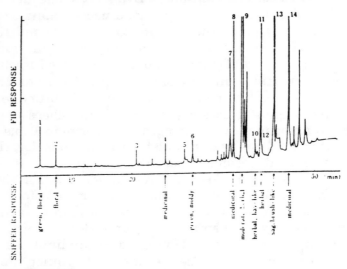

Sesquiterpenoids:

1, *Linalool ($C_{10}H_{18}O$)*

2, *Terpinene-4-ol ($C_{10}H_{18}O$)*

4, *Unknown peak No. 23*

6, *Humulene epoxide II ($C_{15}H_{24}O$)*

7, *Unknown peak No. 41 ($C_{15}H_{24}O$)*

8, *Unknown peak No. 42 ($C_{15}H_{24}O$)*

9, *T-cadinol ($C_{15}H_{24}O$)*

10, *Unknown peak No. 44 ($C_{15}H_{24}O$)*

11, *Unknown peak No. 46 ($C_{15}H_{24}O$)*

12, *Unknown peak No. 47*

13, *Humulenol II ($C_{15}H_{24}O$)*

14, *Unknown peak No. 49 ($C_{15}H_{24}O$)*

sensory character of this hop!

My first reaction to this was one of disappointment. How can we develop rational strategies for hop usage when such little things have such a big effect? But the more I thought about this, the more my opinion shifted. First of all, it absolutely decimates the notion that beer is a simple, one-dimensional libation. For example, hops can run circles around grapes anyday with respect to complexity and subtlety. This also underscores the idea that the more we understand about beer and its constituents, the greater our respect for this natural and wonderful food product.

Dr. George Fix, a professor of science, is an acknowledged brewing expert and consultant, and the author of numerous articles on beer. His new book, An Introduction to Brewing Science, *will be published in 1989 by Brewers Publications.*

A beer-lovers dream:
a beer that is bigger than the thirst.

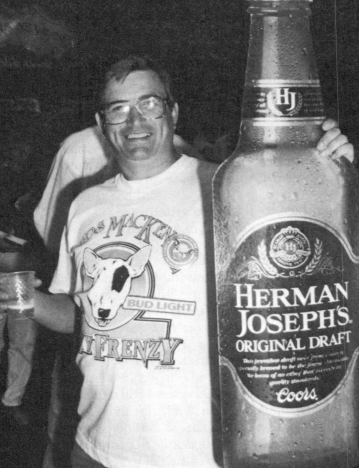

12.
Beer Formulation

Daniel J. Carey
Project Engineer, JV Northwest, Inc.

I was asked to speak about beer formulations and have decided to concentrate on one beer style for the sake of thoroughness. I will describe how I would develop a recipe for a Maibock, which is essentially a pale bock beer. In German, *Mai* means May. In Bavaria, the end of winter is celebrated on May First with a festival. Those of you from Wisconsin may be familiar with this May festival. Most breweries in Bavaria brew a Maibock beer specifically for that spring festival.

As a pale beer, Maibock is golden to pale amber in color. That corresponds to about 5 to 10 degrees Lovibond, and as you probably know, Lovibond is a way of calibrating color, just as Fahrenheit degrees calibrate temperature. To give you a reference point, Miller Lite has a color of about 3.2 degrees Lovibond. Budweiser is 2.7; Pilsner Urquel is 5; a typical Oktoberfest might be 10 to 20 degrees Lovibond, and Guinness comes in around 70. So you can

see that Maibock is not as dark as you might expect for a bock beer.

Maibock

Golden to pale amber color
(5 to 10 degrees Lovibond)

Full flavored but mild
Original Gravity 16 to 18 degrees Plato
5 to 5.5% Alcohol by weight

High-hopping rate to balance sweetness
25 to 33 Bitterness Units

Maibock does have the high gravity of a bock beer. In Germany a bock beer must be between 16 and 18 degrees Plato (P) original gravity. For those of you who don't normally deal in degrees Plato, one degree of Plato is approximately equivalent to four specific gravity units. Therefore, a beer of 16 degrees P would have a specific gravity of 1.064. A Maibock is typically 5 to 5.5 percent alcohol by weight.

Maibock is a full-flavored beer, very drinkable, and well balanced. The key, I believe (which incidentally is the key to making a lot of good beers), is not to overdo the maltiness nor the hop bitterness, but to strive for a nice marriage. No matter how heavy the beer is or what its bitterness units are, as long as it is well balanced, you will have a very drinkable beer. Because Maibock has such a high original gravity, it needs a relatively high hopping rate to balance the malty sweetness. That corresponds to

25 to 33 Bitterness Units.

Let's say, for the sake of example, that you were preparing for a homebrew competition and wanted to copy Spaten Maibock. This is a very popular beer with an original gravity and alcohol within the accepted range. The beer color is pale amber.

Spaten Maibock

Original Gravity (degrees Plato)	16.2
Alcohol (wt/wt)	5.26
Color (degrees Lovibond)	6.2
Apparent Extract (degrees Plato)	3.9
Real Extract (degrees Plato)	6.24
Real Degree of Fermentation	61.8%
Protein (N x 6.25)	0.67%
Bitterness Units	30
C02 (volume)	2.65
pH	4.67
Calories (per 12 oz.)	216

Depending on raw materials, mashing, method and yeast, between 50 and 75 percent of a beer wort is fermentable. Low alcohol beers are made by using a sugar rest temperature of around 163 degrees F and a low original gravity (typically 7 to 8 degrees P). This high mash temperature quickly destroys most of the beta amylase leaving only limited alpha amylase activity and thus the wort fermentability approaches the minimum value of 50 percent. The 75 percent fermentability corresponds to a very low mash sugar rest temperature, for example, 144 degrees F. Of course, you wouldn't achieve a

Daniel Carey

sufficient extract using a single temperature infusion at this low temperature. A typical American beer will have a degree of fermentability close to 65 percent. Spaten Maibock's real degree of fermentability is 62 percent—slightly lower than the typical beer that would be expected for a beer of 16 degrees P. A sugar rest temperature of 156 degrees F and a fast ramp up from protein rest will guarantee a relatively low degree of fermentability.

At 67 percent, the protein level of Spaten Maibock isn't high, considering that this beer has an original gravity of 16.2. Because our beer will be brewed with American malt that typically has 10 to 20 percent more protein than German malt, we could use 20 percent adjunct to more closely approximate the Spaten Maibock protein level. Adjuncts are not bad ingredients. If you have tasted an Augsburger Bock beer, you know that it is a very rich, full-flavored beer, even though it has about 20 percent corn. However, in order to be more traditional, we will not use an adjunct.

In making beer, the first thing to consider is water. Water makes up 90 percent of beer, so let's consider water from a brewing standpoint and what treatment will make it acceptable for Maibock beer.

Hardness refers to the level of calcium and magnesium salts in water. Hardness is made up of permanent hardness and temporary hardness. Temporary hardness is precipitated by boiling and comprises calcium magnesium bicarbonate We don't want high temporary hardness. Permanent hardness is salts of calcium/magnesium and chlorides or sulfates. Permanent hardness is beneficial to sound brewing. (See "calcium" below.)

Alkalinity. We will consider alkalinity as temporary hardness. For pale beer, we like to have alkalinity below 100 parts per million and below 50 if possible.

Calcium. Calcium, as many of you know, is a brewer's friend. There are a lot of reasons why calcium is helpful in brewing beer, the main reason being that calcium helps lower the mash and wort pH to an acceptable range by reacting with phosphates and proteins in the mash. This helps give a faster runoff in lautering and will fight the tendency to extract astringency from the grains. Calcium aids in enzyme reactions and protects mash enzymes, especially alpha amylase. Calcium also aids in yeast flocculation. Fifty to 100 parts per million are necessary for good pale bocks.

Sodium. Salt (NaCl) over 150 parts per million

produces a salty flavor in beer. Brewers used to add sodium chloride to their beer to give the illusion of fullness and sweetness. However, I don't recommend doing that.

Sulfate contributes to the dry, bitter flavor of beer.

Chlorides contribute to palate fullness and sweetness. In Bavaria, calcium chloride is a typical additive to brewing water.

Magnesium. In mild beers, more than 50 parts per million magnesium is astringent, and in the presence of high sulfate—for example, 125 parts per million—it can act as a laxative. I don't know why anyone would want to add magnesium sulfate to a beer.

Los Angeles Water Treatment

	L.A Water	After Dilution w/ Distilled	Add CaCl2
Total Hardness (as CaCO3)	234	117	242
Alkalinity (as CaCO3)	131	65	65
Calcium (ppm)	57	29	79
Sodium (ppm)	60	30	30
Magnesium (ppm)	22	11	11
Sulfate (ppm)	158	79	79
Chloride (ppm)	54	27	115

Water
Pretend, for this discussion, that you live in Los Angeles. As a result, your water is medium hard but acceptable for Maibock beer.

At over 100, the alkalinity is a problem because it

has a tendency to keep the pH of the mash high. This will extract astringency from the grain and also will overshadow the delicate bitterness from the hops. If you have ever tasted a beer that has been made with very alkaline water, you may have noticed a sharp bitterness. One method for lowering alkalinity is to treat the water with lime. This is common in some of the smaller Bavarian breweries. Lime is calcium hydroxide. By raising the pH of the water, lime causes the calcium bicarbonate to precipitate out as calcium carbonate.

Our Water
1) Medium Hard. Slightly high but acceptable.
2) Alkalinity. Too high for a pale beer.
>   Methods to lower alkalinity:
>   Lime treatment
>   Acidify to pH 6.5 to 6.8
>   Counteract with Calcium addition
>   Boiling
>   Ion Exchange
>   Dilution

3) Calcium. Slightly low. Can add $CaCl_2$. Sulfur is too high to add $CaSO_4$. $CaCl_2$ will contribute to malty fullness.
4) Sodium. High but acceptable.
5) Sulfate. Relatively high. No addition of $CaSO_4$.

Treatment of Our Water
1) Dilute 50/50 with distilled water
2) Add $CaCl_2$.
>   140 ppm $CaCl_2$ will contribute 50 ppm Ca^{++} and
>   88 ppm Cl^-. 140 ppm $CaCl_2$ = .52 grams/gal.
>   1 grain/gal. = 17.1 ppm

Daniel J. Carey

Another method of lowering the alkalinity is treating your water with acid, but this is too dangerous for the homebrewer. A brewer may opt to use ion exchange to lower alkalinity, although for the homebrewer, ion exchange is too complicated and too expensive to be practical. The simplest way to lower the alkalinity in a five-gallon batch of beer is to dilute the water with distilled water. At a rate of one dollar per gallon, you can buy distilled water and lower the alkalinity very effectively.

In making a dark bock beer, the alkalinity isn't such a problem. Roasted malts have a natural acidity that helps counteract any alkalinity. However, when you are making a dark beer with alkaline water, you need to keep your hopping rate low because the alkalinity will not only extract harshness from the grain, but it will also produce a sharp, astringent bitterness from the hop that is not desirable.

The calcium is slightly low in the L. A. water. Adding calcium chloride (CaCl2) will increase the calcium level and contribute to that malty fullness we are looking for. The sulfate content of the water is too high to add calcium sulfate (CaSO4)

The sodium is a little high but acceptable.

As I indicated above, the simplest way to treat water is to dilute it with distilled water. If we dilute it fifty/fifty, the alkalinity will drop down into an acceptable range. All we have to do at that point is to add some calcium chloride. By adding 50 parts per million calcium, the calcium level would rise to 80 parts per million. At 140 parts per million, calcium chloride will contribute 50 parts per million calcium and about 90 parts per million of chloride. That 140 parts per million of calcium chloride is equivalent to about .5 grams per gallon. One grain per gallon equals 17.1 parts per million.

If we hadn't treated this water we would have had to decrease the hopping rate for reasons I have explained. In the end, the alkalinity would have ruined the delicate flavor of this beer.

Malt

Now let's consider malt. To copy this Maibock requires a wort original gravity of 16.2 degrees Plato. This is equivalent to 44 pounds of extract per barrel. This number was arrived at as follows:

259* x specific gravity x degrees P divided by 100 =
pounds extract per barrel
(*one barrel of water weighs 259 pounds)

In our case, this is as follows:
259 x 1.064 x 16/100 = 44 pounds

If we assume that 62 percent brewhouse extraction is typical for a homebrewer (that is 62 percent of the total grain weight finds its way into the cold wort), dividing 44 pounds extract by 62 percent efficiency, we find that we will need 72 pounds of grain per barrel of finished beer, or 2.3 pounds per gallon, or 11.5 pounds per five-gallon batch.

Malt Used

Type	% Used	Pounds for five gallons
Pale	78	9.00
Dextrin	10	1.15

| Munich | 10 | 1.15 |
| Caramel | 2 | 0.20 |

Total   11.5 pounds

 The bulk of our grains will be pale malt. We will also use dextrin, which contributes to mouthfeel, palate fullness, and foam stability. We will add a little Munich malt to contribute to the maltiness of the beer—a very important quality in Bavarian-style beer. Last comes a little caramel malt to add complexity and depth.

 Specialty malt should only be used if it is fresh in order to contribute positive flavor aroma to the beer. Avoid using old malt.

 As for the color of Maibock, there is no scientific, consistent way of taking the color of your malt and converting that into the color of your finished beer. There are too many variables. Based on experience in your brewhouse, you can determine what malts and brewing methods will produce a given beer color. I know that the above combination will produce a pale amber beer at about 6 degrees Lovibond.

Q: What is dextrin malt?
A: Dextrin malt is a type of roasted malt. Basically, wet, green malt after germination is held at about 150 degrees F so that in each grain a little mashing occurs. The endosperm starch is transformed into unfermentable dextrins. The only difference between caramel malt and dextrin malt is that upon kilning, the caramel malt is brought up to a much higher temperature to develop color. The dextrin malt is not dried at such a high temperature,

and therefore it doesn't develop the same level of color.

Q: Most of us don't have access to dextrin malt..
A: Sure you do. Dextrin malt is sometimes called carapils.

Hops
Maibock is a Bavarian-style beer so we need to stick with the German aromatics completely.

Hops
German Tettnanger at 4% alpha
German Hallertau Mittlefruh at 4% alpha
Use as 50/50 blend
When to Add Hops for a 90-Minute Boil
Start of boil 25%
At 30 minutes 50%
End of boil 25%

I like to use a fifty/fifty blend of Tettnangers and Mittlefruh, and I assume that by the time we get these hops, they both have a 4 percent alpha average. I use a typical ninety-minute boil adding 25 percent of the hops at the start, 50 percent at thirty minutes and 25 percent at the end. The reason hops are traditionally added at the start of the boil is to prevent boiling over. You homebrewers know that a five-gallon batch of beer can boil over and make a mess in the kitchen. But when a 500-hectoliter brew kettle starts foaming over, it is a hazard.

The recipe for Spaten calls for 30 Bitterness Units. How much hops shall we add to achieve that? Bitterness Units, of course, are milligrams per liter, so I can calculate the desired Bitterness Units as follows:

Daniel J. Carey

How Much Hops to Achieve 30 Bitterness Units

$$\text{grams/hl} = \frac{\text{Bitterness Units desired}}{\frac{\% \text{ alpha}}{100}} \times \frac{\text{recovery efficiency}}{100} \times \frac{1,000 \text{ mg/gm}}{100 \text{ l/hl}}$$

$$\text{equals } \frac{30 \text{ BU}}{.04 \times .25 \times 10} \text{ equals } 300 \text{ gm/hl}$$

$$\frac{300 \text{ gm/hl}}{387.8} \text{ equals } 0.77 \text{ lbs./bbl} = 2 \text{ oz. } / 5 \text{ gal.}$$

Efficiencies seem to be about 20 to 35 percent, which means that for every 100 parts of alpha acids you buy, you will end up with only 20 to 35 parts left in the beer. This makes 300 grams per hectoliter. With my formula that converts grams per hectoliter to pounds per barrel, I can figure that this equals two ounces per five-gallon batch.

Bitterness units in themselves don't really mean much. A light beer with 30 Bitterness Units would be extremely bitter. However, 30 Bitterness Units at 16 degrees P produce a very well-balanced beer.

Mash

To determine our mash thickness, we must decide how much water and grain to use. I have included here some numbers for a typical infusion mash, American double mash, and decoction mash.

Mash Thickness

Infusion Mash: .18 to .36 gallons water per pound of malt
American Double Mash: .25 to .36 gallons water per pound
    of malt.
Decoction Mash: .36 to .6 gallons water per pound of malt

   To make Maibock, we will be doing a single decoction mash. Because of the large amount of malt necessary, I have chosen to use .36 gallons of water per pound of malt. That gives us 4.1 gallons of water plus 11.5 pounds of malt to go into our mash tun.

   .36 gal. water / lb. malt x 11.5 lb. malt = 4.1 gal. water

   When I worked in Germany, for example, for our Maibock, we used the 0.36 figure, and with Pils a 0.52 figure, and they were both single decoctions.
   As a side note: beer that has gone through a decoction program has been mixed, boiled, and pumped. Therefore, the grain has lost its buoyancy and has a tendency to sink onto the false bottom like cement, thus making the lauter process difficult. Rakes in the lauter tun lift and split the bed to facilitate lautering. In an infusion mash tun, however, the grain is neither pumped nor mixed. Therefore, rakes are not necessary in the infusion lauter tun. The mash has a high buoyancy and is much easier to run off.

Volume
   We know how much grain we are going to use, and we know how much water we are going to require. What

Daniel J. Carey

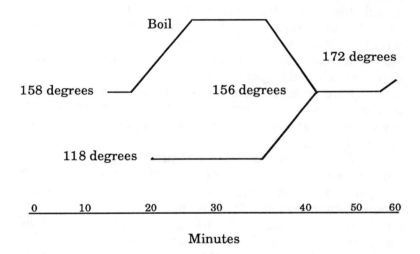

volume does that correspond to? One pound of malt displaces .08 gallons of water. That means that 11.5 pounds of malt times .08 gallons per pound equals .9 gallons. Therefore, our total mash volume is 5 gallons, that is .9 gallons of malt plus 4.1 gallons of water. It takes five gallons of mash to make a five-gallon brew.

Mash Program
Next we will decide on a mash program.

With all-malt beer, using American malts, protein rests aren't critical. When you make all-malt beer, there is plenty of nitrogen available for the yeast. With American malts, about 70 percent of the available nitrogen is produced during malting. Only about 30 percent more is gained with a protein rest. What that means is that an all-malt beer made with American malt with no protein rest has about the same nitrogen as a brew made with 70 percent malt and 30 percent adjunct, using a protein rest.

I am going to take 40 percent of my mash and 40 percent of the water, bring the temperature to 156 degrees, and rest for ten minutes, working up to a boil relatively fast.

In the meantime, I am going to take the other 60 percent of the mash and water to perform a short protein rest in the lauter tun. The protein rest is necessary because when I combine the two mashes, I can achieve my sugar rest temperature of 156 degrees F, which I will hold for twenty minutes. I can add external heat or boiling water to reach 172 degrees F for mash off. Why is a "mash off" step necessary? It not only destroys most of the malt enzymes, thus fixing the wort chemistry, it also increases extraction efficiency. Not all malt starches gelatinize at the lower sugar rest temperature. Gelatinization is the process by which the starch granules burst open so that the malt enzymes can act upon them. Different starch granules gelatinize over different temperature ranges. The 172 degrees F rest allows for a little more gelatinization and alpha amylase activity in order to eke out a little bit more extract.

Q: What would happen if you were making an infusion

mash and went to a really high temperature of 180 degrees F?

A: For one thing, it would denature all of the alpha amylase so that you would get an extremely starchy, hazy wort that probably wouldn't even run off.

A few brewers have found that even though the decoction mash takes a lot of extra time and effort, it is important in making their beer better. And if you are going to enter your beer in a competition, you will want to do anything you can to make your beer even 2 percent better. However, there are a lot of perfectly good beers that are made with single-temperature infusions.

How do I know that by boiling 40 percent of the grain and combining it with the other 60 percent at a protein rest temperature that I am going to achieve 156 degrees F?

Let's figure the temperature of the protein rest to achieve 156 degrees F for sugar rest.

1 pound of malt contains the same amount of heat as .05 gallons of water

Therefore:

Malt heat equivalent
= .05 gallons / 1 lb. x 11.5 lb
= .6 heat equivalent

Total mash heat equivalent
= .6 gal. + 4.1 gal.
= 4.7 gal.

40% decoction   = .4 x 4.7 gal. = 1.9 gal. equivalent
60% main mash = .6 x 4.7 gal. = 2.8 gal. equivalent

Therefore:

Aa   +Bb   Cc
1.9 (212F)   +2.8 (x)   4.7 (156F)
x = 118 F protein rest temperature

Sparge

Sparging is typically anywhere from 0.37 to 0.5 gallons per pound of malt used. We will stay toward the low end of the sparging.

Fermentation and Lager

One can argue about hops, malts, and temperatures all day, but the difference between a great beer and a good beer can be your choice of yeast. Fermentation is extremely important. Beer is a product of yeast. If you taste wort and then taste beer, you realize what a dramatic effect yeast has on the flavor of beer. If I were going to make a Maibock for a competition, I would want to use the yeast strain 34/70, which is available from the Weihenstephan yeast bank. You may write to them at

Weihenstephan Hefe Bank
D-8050
Freising 12
West Germany

This strain also is available in the U.S. from Wyeast Labs in Mount Hood, Oregon.

I will finish by talking about typical fermentation temperatures. For a Maibock, a traditional fermentation program could begin at 48 degrees F, rising to 53 degrees until 10 percent fermentable extract remains. The apparent gravity should be 5.25 degrees P. At this point, transfer the beer to the cellar to ferment down that last little bit of extract and build up the carbonation. Hold the beer at 32 degrees F for eight weeks.

Q: Is there much difference in the CO_2 level between German and American beers?
A: No. The level of CO_2 is not really any higher in either beer.

Q: One more question: At what temperature do you pitch the yeast during primary fermentation?
A: I would pitch at about 48 degrees F using, of course, a strong yeast able to ferment at cold temperatures. The period of primary fermentation is from five to eight days.

Daniel Carey is project manager for J.V. Northwest Inc., and a consultant to the microbrewing and pubbrewing industry. He graduated from the University of California at Davis in 1982 with a degree in Food Science and Technology with emphasis in Malting and Brewing Science. He is a graduate of the Siebel Institute where he was the 1987 class Valedictorian. He has brewed at the Ayinger Brauerei in Bavaria.

Dictionary of Beer and Brewing

Just released, this valuable reference will make an outstanding contribution to any brewing library! Author Carl Forget has compiled 1,929 essential definitions used in beer-making, including: • Brewing Processes • Ingredients • Types and Styles of Beer • Abbreviations • Arcane Terms • Also: Conversion Tables for temperatures, alcohol percentages, and factors.

Members $15.95 / Nonmembers $19.95
6 x 9, 196 pp.

Brewing Lager Beer

This classic reference book is a must for serious brewers interested in all-grain brewing and recipes. First, author Greg Noonan describes the brewing process and ingredients in plain English. Then he guides you through planning and brewing seven classic lager beers — including recipes. As a bonus, the tables of brewing information are excellent.

Members $12.95 / Nonmembers $14.95
5 1/2 x 8 1/2, 320 pp.

Best of Beer & Brewing

From the transcripts of the 1982-1985 Conferences on Beer and Brewing

Rather than reprint all four transcripts, we chose the very best 15 talks from the four Conferences, asked the authors to update and correct them, and compiled them in one valuable, affordable volume.

Members $15.95 / Nonmembers $17.95
5 1/2 x 8 1/2, 208 pp.

Beer and Brewing, Vol. 6

Transcript of the 1986 Conference on Quality Beer and Brewing

A practical collection of 20 chapters from some of the most knowledgeable brewing experts in the U.S. Topics include: Training to Perceive Flavor • Brewing Light Lager • Cultivation and Use of Hops • The Magic of Malt • Brewing Water: Its Effect on Flavor • Yeast Usage, and fourteen more.

Members $18.95 / Nonmembers $20.95
5 1/2 x 8 1/2, 260 pp.

Beer and Brewing, Vol. 7

Transcript of the 1987 Conference on Quality Beer and Brewing

This collection gives readers the widest range of beer information ever published in a single volume. Suited for commercial and homebrewers. Its 17 chapters include: Yeast Strain Traits • Recipe Formulation • Brewing to Scale • Brewing in Your Environs • Origin of Beer Flavor • Innovations in Equipment • Beer Folklore • Contemporary Brewing • Plus ten more.

Members $18.95 / Nonmembers $20.95
5 1/2 x 8 1/2, 280 pp.

All prices are quoted in U.S. Dollars in 1988. Prices may change and shipping charges vary. For information, write or call: Association of Brewers, PO Box 287, Boulder, CO 80306 USA. Tel. 303/447-0816.

ZYMURGY Magazine

A magazine dedicated to homebrewers and beer lovers. The quality of information is so good that many professional brewers subscribe. Articles are entertaining and informative on brewing, beer recipes, history and styles. One year's subscription includes five 64-page issues annually, plus membership in the American Homebrewers Association.

1 year $21.00 / 2 years $38.00 / 3 years $57.00   Foreign add US $5.

Brewery Operations, Vol. 3
1986 Microbrewers Transcript

The Brewery Operations series books provide practical, tried-and-true suggestions for small-scale brewing and marketing. Chapters include: Wort Production • Marketing the Pubbrewery • Contract Brewing • Yeast and Fermentation • Brewery Public Relations • Cottage Brewing • and more.

5 1/2 x 8 1/2, 180 pp.   **Member $23.95 / Nonmember $25.95**

Brewery Operations, Vol. 4
1987 Microbrewers Conference Transcript

The 1987 Conference held in Boston was the best to date, and Volume 4 provides you with its expert information on brewing, marketing, engineering and management. Chapters include: Malt Extract in Microbrewing • Techniques of Major Breweries • Engineering for the Microbrewer • Developing a Marketing Plan • How to Hire Good People • Equipment Systems for the Brewpub • BATF Regulations, and much more.

5 1/2 x 8 1/2, 210 pp.   **Member $23.95 / Nonmember $25.95**

North American
Microbrewers Resource Handbook and Directory 1988

We know how valuable this book has been to the industry by the thousands we have sold. This year, we've had to expand the 1988 MRH by more than one-third to handle the added information we've included. Here are the updated telephone numbers, addresses, personnel, and descriptions of North American breweries and suppliers. Lists: Micros and Brewpubs of North America • Ingredient Suppliers • Brewing Consultants • Equipment Manufacturers • Large Breweries • Associations and Publications • State Laws and Excise Taxes • and so much more.

Plus, "A Guide to Opening a Small Brewery," a comprehensive list of questions for startup or expansion.

8 1/2 x 11, 336 pp.   **Members $35.00 / Nonmembers $45.00**

The New Brewer

The New Brewer is designed to address the needs of the serious, small-scale commercial brewer. We provide up-to-date facts about: • Technical Data on Brewing • Reports on Brewing Equipment • Marketing Strategies • Beer Styles Worldwide • Current Industry News • Legal and Tax Issues •Public Relations • New Product Reviews • Profiles of Breweries • Employee Management • Brewery Safety • And much more.

50 pages per issue. Published six times yearly.

$48/Year (US) $58/Year (Foreign)